The Visitor Experience at the Mark Twain House

The Visitor Experience at the Mark Twain House

Stephanie C. Fox

QueenBeeBooks

Bloomfield, Connecticut, U.S.A.

Copyright © April 12, 2020 by Stephanie C. Fox

All rights reserved. Published in the United States by QueenBeeBooks, Connecticut.

Library of Congress Cataloging-in-Publication Data
Name: Fox, Stephanie C., author.
Title: The Visitor Experience at the Mark Twain House. / Stephanie C. Fox.
Description: Connecticut: QueenBeeBooks, [2011].
Library of Congress Control Number: 2020906622
Identifiers: ISBN: 978-1-7343743-6-0 (paperback)
Subjects: 1. United States – State & Local – New England (CT) —History. 2. United States – Northeast – New England (CT) —Travel. 3. Historic Preservation – General—Architecture.

www.queenbeeedit.com

Cover design by Stephanie C. Fox
Cover photograph by Stephanie C. Fox
Printed in the United States of America

This book is dedicated to the many museum people who get to know the public daily:

Visitor center staff, which includes, but is not limited to, administrators, schedulers, gift shop personnel, and tour guides, or, as we are referred to at the Mark Twain House, historic interpreters.

Most particularly, I dedicate this book to Vera E.R. Klein, who was the Visitor Center Director when I was a historic interpreter in the 1990s. She was wonderful to work with, and is a wonderful person and friend.

Also by Stephanie C. Fox

The Book of Thieves

The Bear Guarding the Beehive

Nae-Née
Birth Control: Infallible, with
Nanites and Convenience for All

Vaccine: The Cull
Nae-Née Wasn't Enough

New World Order Underwater
The Nae-Née Inventors Strike Back

What the Small Gray Visitor Said

Elephant's Kitchen
– An Aspergirl's Study in Difference

Almost a Meal –
A True Tale of Horror

Scheherazade Cat:
The Story of a War Hero

An American Woman in Kuwait

Hawai'i – Stolen Paradise:
A Travelogue

Hawai'i – Stolen Paradise:
A Brief History

Table of Contents

Acknowledgements iii
Preface v

Part One: The Tour

Outside the House 3
The Drawing Room 15
The Dining Room 20
The Servants' Hall and Butler's Pantry 24
The Library 25
The Mahogany Guest Suite 29
Back in the Front Hall, at the Stairwell 31
Olivia's Sewing Alcove 32
Sam and Olivia's Room 33
Suzy's Room 37
Outside Katy Leary's Sewing Room 39
The Grandmother's Room 40
The School Room 41
Clara and Jean's Room 44
The Third Floor 46
The Billiards Room 49
After Life in the Hartford House 55

Part Two: The Making of a Historic Interpreter

Training 61
Field Trip to Elmira, New York 66
Reading List 74

Part Three: The Questions People Ask…

    Questions…and Answers 79

Part Four: Visitor Services of All Kinds

    Visitor Services and Other Facts 91
    The Visitor Center and Gift Shop 94
    Additional Services 101

About the Author 103

Acknowledgements

No writer can claim to have produced any book completely on her (or his) own, with no help from anyone else. I would like to thank everyone who helped me with this project. I thank my mother, Carole B. C. Fox, for her input concerning the content of the book and for putting me in touch with a great editor. And I thank my father, Paul W. Fox, for enduring hours of seemingly endless frustration with the computer. Without his patience and time, this book would not have been written. My uncle, Douglas A. Conant, spent many late hours on the phone with me and with my father, straightening out the messes we have made with something that, no doubt, Mark Twain would also have considered a maddening piece of machinery.

Several people assisted and encouraged me with the content of this book. Emojean Weaver, a great editor, patiently read my single-spaced rough draft, and showed me around her fascinating home, which is like a colonial historic house museum. Her husband, Professor Glenn Weaver, shared the benefit of his experience as a writer and published author with me. Ernest Shaw, owner of Heritage Trails, a tour company, told me how he went about publishing his own work. He also drove eight of us – all Mark Twain House historic interpreters – to Elmira, New York on Mothers' Day to see where Mark Twain spent the other half of his time for seventeen years. Beverly Zell, the photograph librarian at the Mark Twain House, helped me to sift through the collection, and graciously produced copies of photographs with background information.

The historic interpreters at the Mark Twain House read what I wrote, pronounced it acceptable for publication, and are great fun to work with. The experience of working with them has been invaluable, for their friendship as well as for everything I learned from them. They have taught me not only history, but also how to address groups both as a lecturer and as a conversationalist who interprets the past.

Of course, I must thank Mark Twain, or, as we like to refer to him, Sam – for providing such hilarious, uproarious, continuously relevant, and fascinating subject matter. His comments about life will never be out of date.

And, not the least, I thank my grandmother, Barbara M. R. Conant, for suggesting that I apply to work at the Mark Twain House as a historic interpreter. That has proven to be some of the best advice I have ever received.

Preface

Mark Twain once wrote that an introduction is an author's justification for having written a book, thus disclaiming any need for one. I agree with him. Often, introductions come across as boring and monotonous, and the reader feels only obligated to read that part of the book, if even that.

So, I will simply address one issue – briefly. That issue is the title of this book.

There is a specific reason why I have titled this book *The Visitor Experience* at the Mark Twain House. The term "the visitor experience" is used by people who have had contact with aliens. Not foreigners – aliens (people or beings from other planets). In service-oriented businesses, one deals with aliens of a different kind: strangers from our own planet. These strangers are not merely from other countries, cultures, or religions. They come from other states, towns, cities, families, walks of life, professions, values, and experiences. Each person is the sum of these experiences and attributes.

A guide must be prepared to encounter someone completely different each and every time that she or he goes out to face a new group of visitors. The guides' assumptions must therefore be kept to a minimum, and nothing may be taken for granted. Our assumptions are challenged with each new visitor experience, and that is part of what keeps our jobs interesting.

I have found that the most effective way to have a successful encounter with a stranger is to accept that she or he may be as different from me – inside – as an alien from another planet would be. This analogy has served me well at the Mark Twain House.

This book contains a tour that I gave as a historic interpreter at the Mark Twain House in Hartford, Connecticut. It takes the readers from the front lawn to the porch to the hall, then goes room by room throughout the author's family home, telling the story of the wonderful life they all lived in a house that felt alive to them for seventeen years.

I did this for several years, and it enabled me to learn all about the author and his family, and to read many of his works. It also led me to meet many fascinating and fun members of the public as I showed them around and told them hilarious, uproarious tales of Samuel Langhorne Clemens, a.k.a. Mark Twain, in the manner of a stand-up comic. They loved it, as did I.

Many of these visitors made a wonderful remark to me at the conclusion of tour after tour after tour: "That was the best tour I have ever had anywhere. I wish I could buy a copy of it. You should write your tour down, as is." So, I did.

Part One: *The Tour*

Outside the House

Welcome to Nook Farm. This is all that remains of it – three houses and two carriage houses. There were eighteen homes here in the late nineteenth century, and they all sat in the nook, or curve, of the Park River, which was off to the southwest. That nook has been buried, along with most of the river. The homes had all the modern conveniences of their time, including indoor plumbing, running hot water, central heating, and gas lighting – provided by the Hartford Gas Company.

Most of the people who lived here were authors, lawyers and political activists – and there was Charles Dudley Warner, the editor of *The Hartford Courant*. Of course, the two most famous residents of Nook Farm were Harriet Beecher Stowe and Mark Twain. That, through the trees, is the back door of Mrs. Stowe's cottage-style mansion. It qualifies as a mansion because it has a front and a back staircase. She moved there in 1873, when she was 62 years old and had already been world-famous for twenty-one years for writing *Uncle Tom's Cabin*.

The following year, Mark Twain moved to this house. It was 1874, he was 39 years old, and he was not yet world-famous. That would come two years later, when he wrote *The Adventures of Tom Sawyer*. He came to Hartford because his publisher and business contacts were here, and because a college friend of his wife's lived in the neighborhood.

His real name was Samuel Langhorne Clemens. He adopted the penname "Mark Twain" in 1863, after having worked for a few years as a Mississippi River steamboat pilot. Look at the shape of the house: it looks sort of like a Mississippi River steamboat. This is a coincidence. Mark Twain hadn't yet written anything about steamboats in *Tom Sawyer*, *Huckleberry Finn*, or *Life on the Mississippi* when this house was being designed, but this makes a very convenient tool for explaining his penname. The architect did not know that Sam had been a steamboat pilot – he was just having fun with the design. Notice the Texas-deck, and the front porch, or veranda.

On the steamboats, the pilothouses, like this Texas-deck, were two stories up, surrounded by glass, and the steering and navigation apparatus was inside those and only those. So, there was no way from up there to measure the depth of the water. Someone else, down at the front of the boat, had to do that, using a metal weight on a long rope with a mark on it – such as a knot – to mark off the desired depth. When the water rose up to the mark or higher, the person would shout "By the Mark Twain!" up to the pilot, who would then know that it was safe to go on. A fathom is six feet deep, and two of these make a twain, so they were literally marking the twain. They had to get this right, because if they didn't, and the boat continued on down the river, it could run aground and blow up. Sam lost his younger brother Henry this way – on a boat that someone else was piloting – so of course he understood how important it was to measure the depth correctly. I will refer to the author as Sam and Mark Twain throughout the tour.

His wife's name was Olivia Louise Langdon Clemens. I'll refer to her as Olivia. She was born and brought up in Elmira, New York. Her father died in 1870, several months after she was married, and left her a quarter of a million dollars. She spent $100,000 of it on this house, carriage house, and five and a half acres of land--most of which stretched over this ravine and back toward the nook of the Park River. In those days, if you spent $10,000 on your home, you were spending lots of money, so this was incredible. And she held legal title to this property, as by this time the Women's and Married Women's Property Acts had begun to be passed (Connecticut's was passed in 1877). Sam was already making money from books and lectures, and he would continue to make more money from them. He did own a greenhouse on that sort of hump in the grass behind you. Today it's in Massachusetts; someone bought it a long time ago.

Have a look at the house. The style is High Victorian Gothic, and the architect's name was Edward Tuckerman Potter. He designed churches as well as houses. We'll see some evidence of that inside. Potter had a record time--just sixteen months--to oversee the construction of the house while Sam and Olivia traveled in England and Scotland and Sam lectured. Before they left, Olivia spoke to the architect. She told him that she wanted two things. She wanted a guestroom on the first floor (rather unusual) and she wanted the house to face this way – to the grass, the trees and the other houses instead of the street, which was a dirt road covered with horse manure. She didn't want to look at that. The servants' wing ended up facing the street. That's all either of them said, and then they left. And this is what they found when they returned. They were ideal clients...perfectly satisfied with the distinctive result that their architect had prepared for them.

The neighbors had a lot to say about it. They couldn't understand why such an "outrageous, flamboyant and unusual-looking structure" wasn't facing them – but Olivia had her reasons. They called the black and vermilion paint markings "tattoo markings." And Mr. Franklin Chamberlain, a Hartford lawyer, state legislator and land speculator, was building his retirement home across the yard (now the Stowe-Day Library). During its construction, he kept saying that when he was done, he'd show Mark Twain what good taste was (though he would really be showing the architect). Of course, you can judge for yourselves. Mark Twain did. Three years after he moved in (1877), he wrote a poem about the house for *The Traveler's Record*. Here is the first verse:

This is the house that Mark built.
These are the bricks of various hue
And shape and position, straight and askew,
With its nooks and angles and gables too,
Which make up the house presented to view,
The curious house that Mark built.

Even though he didn't build it.

It used to have ivy growing very thickly all over the veranda, and rose bushes outside. The rose was Olivia's favorite flower. We still have her original wisteria bush by the porte-cochere. It grows long, drooping, heavily perfumed purple flowers in the late spring and early summer.

Eleven cats and four dogs lived here. They were allowed in both buildings. Sam loved cats. He collected them wherever he lived. This was a habit that ran in his family. At one point, his mother, Jane Lampton Clemens, had nineteen cats while living in Hannibal, Missouri. Sam once wrote, "A home without a cat - and a well-fed, well-petted, and properly revered cat – may be a perfect home, perhaps, but how can it prove title?"

There were seven servants. There was a butler. His name was George Griffin, and he was a former slave. After he was married, he lived in town with his wife, Mary, and their daughter. He came to work here each day at the crack of dawn. As he was considered to be a part of the family, his room was in the family quarters of the house, not in the servants' wing or carriage house. He continued to use this room once a week, on Friday nights, after he was married.

The coachman's name was Patrick McAleer. He did the gardening in his spare time. He lived in that right-hand wing of the carriage house with his wife, Ellen, and their seven children.

The other five servants – single women – lived on the second floor of the servants' wing, which faces the street. They were three maids, a German nanny, and a cook.

As for the Clemens family, it consisted of Sam, Olivia, and, before they moved here, their son Langdon Clemens – but he caught diphtheria and died when he was a year and a half old in June of

1872. There was no cure for diphtheria. When the family moved here in September of 1874, Susy was two and a half years old, Clara was a baby, and Jean wasn't born yet. She would follow six years later, in 1880.

Now that you have a cast of human, feline, and canine characters, I will lead you to the front door.

Have a look up. Notice the butterfly and lily cutouts in the woodwork. And behind you and up, in those triangular-shaped openings, you can see three shapes in each: a lily, a bird pecking down at it, and a chipmunk running overhead, towards the bird's tail. The architect wanted to put some nature themes into the project.

Before we go in, there's just one more thing left. I must recite the rules:

Please don't smoke, eat, drink, or chew gum inside.

Please don't take pictures or videos.

Please don't sit on, lean on, or touch anything.

If you get tired, please ask me for a 20th-century, folding chair.

We have some on all three floors.

And please stay with me, in the same room that I am in, at all times.

That's it. You can walk on the floors, and it's all heated/air-conditioned. Now we'll go in. And would the last person in please shut the door – so that no one else can get in. Thank you.

The Front Hall

This is the front entrance hall. The house has 19 rooms, 15 fireplaces, and 7 bathrooms. 3 of the fireplaces and 2 of the bathrooms were in the servants' quarters. The level of light is the same as it was when Mark Twain lived here. He didn't like it. On a gray, overcast day he would complain that it "seemed as if the world was lit by the Hartford Gas Company." Thomas Edison invented the light bulb in 1879, but by then Olivia was settled in, and did not want her house gutted and rewired for electricity, so that wasn't done until the house changed hands in 1903.

In 1881, Olivia hired Louis Comfort Tiffany and his three Associated Artists – Lockwood DeForest, Candace Thurber Wheeler, and Samuel Coleman – from New York City to decorate the first floor and stairwell of the house. The group specialized in Japanese, East Indian, French, Flemish, and Spanish designs, and, as you can see, they used lots of stencilings. This room alone took 40 hours to restore to its original appearance. This is silver paint stenciled on black walnut, dark blue on red, and dark blue and silver on red. The floor is the same white marble tile that the family had, and it has a heat shaft in it. There was a coal furnace in the cellar.

Around the fireplace we have the original carved teakwood imported from India, by Lockwood DeForest. And that's a split chimney – it comes together higher up in the house. We'll see another one like that in the dining room. There used to be a Tiffany stained-glass window in that big empty space, and three more around the front door. They're all gone--the family took them away when they sold the house and left in 1903, and we lost track of them.

We don't know what any of them looked like. Today we keep two inaccurate, Tiffany company guesses on either side of the front door, just so you can see some examples of that company's work. However, thanks to a *Hartford Courant* reporter from the time, I can tell you to some extent what the piece over the fireplace looked like. It was called *Autumn*, it looked like a scene from Lewis Carroll's *Alice in Wonderland*, and it had shades of blue, and some green...but that's all the information we have – not enough to make a reproduction, so we left it blank. If we ever find out exactly how it looked, we will have a new one made and installed. Otherwise, we'll leave it blank.

A lot of the artifacts in the house are original. I will point them out as we go along, starting with this round sofa. Olivia called it a conversation piece, and kept it right here. Off to the side is a music box. It's a period piece, exactly like the one that Clara described in her memoirs. She said that her father brought it home from Switzerland when she was five years old. It was custom-made with the tunes of his choice, and she was delighted with it because it looked like a coffin when closed. When open, it played arias from German and Italian operas and the Lohengrin Wedding March. The butler would wind it up to have it playing music during dinner. It would play for fifteen minutes each time – then he would have to wind it up again. At either side of the room, we have some busts by the artist Karl Gearhart: a black one of Mark Twain in the corner, and a white one by the window of Henry Ward Beecher. Henry Ward Beecher was just two years younger than his famous sister, whom he visited across the yard. He was also famous as a Congregationalist preacher from New York City. He had a large church, which was always packed. He was very popular, very entertaining to listen to, and I will mention him again.

Over here, in a closet, we have a period piece, exactly like the original Butter-Stamp version of the telephone that the family had. [It's shaped like a butter-stamp.] Alexander Graham Bell invented the phone in 1876. A few years later, someone from the company came here to persuade Sam and Olivia to buy one. Now, usually when an opportunity to acquire a new invention came along, Sam really wanted one, and Olivia had doubts. In this case, Olivia really wanted a phone, and Sam had doubts. She thought this would be a great thing to have, in case they needed a doctor for one of their daughters. Sam wasn't so sure, but Olivia always let him buy whatever invention was currently fascinating him, so they bought a telephone. They had it put in the closet in case they didn't like it. After it was installed, Sam's doubts were confirmed when he found that he was paying for a nuisance. The phone kept ringing – or, as it did in those days, buzzing – and demanding attention, so it was nice to be able to shut the door on it. Sam hadn't anticipated that not only would he call people, but that people would also call him.

Here's how it worked: Sam would listen and talk with the attachment below, switching back and forth, and, if he wanted to talk, press the white button above. He preferred to talk. And he would have preferred a 20th-century phone, so he could just call the person he wanted to talk to, and not have an operator connect him every time. So he got very angry with the operators. He called them "hello girls" because they were all women and because they would, not surprisingly, say "hello" when he listened, and he swore at them.

One day, he got himself into trouble. Mrs. Taft, the doctor's wife, a prim, proper neighbor, called Sam. At that exact same moment, Sam went to make a call, so the phone didn't have a chance to ring. Sam listened for, as usual, an instant, promptly heard a female voice saying "hello," and proceeded – according to plan – to start swearing, and loudly. You had to be loud in those days to be heard rather quietly at the other end of the line. Luckily, Olivia was nearby, paying bills in the dining room. She heard everything and rushed over, mortified, with her fingers to her lips. By then, Sam was saying, over and over again, "How many [expletive deleted] times have I got to say 'hello' to you hello girls down there?!!?" Mrs. Taft knew what was going on, but said nothing. She just enjoyed the situation. Meanwhile, Sam noticed Olivia, cleared his throat, and calmly said, never at a loss for words, "I'm sorry, I've had to take the phone away from George, our butler. He's developed a rather nasty habit of swearing lately." He got away with it; George and Mrs. Taft allowed it.

Tacked up on the wall in there is an unused copy, in Sam's handwriting, of the report card he used to send--once a week--to complain about the phone's performance. We don't know whether he got any feedback. But he had a nice system of cross markings: one meant that he heard artillery fire at the receiver, two meant that he heard thunder, three both, and four he wrote "All conditions fail." Nothing – just silence.

Sam later had a chance to invest in the phone, but he turned it down, because he was so annoyed at Alexander Graham Bell for having invented it. Then he saw lots of people buying phones, and he was sorry. He said, "I was never able to recognize an opportunity until it had ceased to be one." But it was just as well that he didn't invest, because that particular phone company later failed. Still, Sam loved gadgets, and he had to have one of each new invention that came out--with the exception of an elevator. It would have required a whole separate building of steam equipment to make it work. He would invest in some things, but not others...never the right things. He would usually break even on these investments, but never make money. Once he lost money – lots of it – but I'll tell you about that invention later.

At first, the only people in Hartford with phones were Mark Twain, the phone company, and the doctor. Later a few businesses had them but because the phone was not a common household appliance, Olivia and the other women of Nook Farm, whether they had careers or not, followed the time-consuming tradition of "calling hours" – so they could keep track of each other on a regular basis. They would stay home on one afternoon per week – always the same one – and receive visitors for 15 minutes each (about the length of a phone call) over tea. Then they would leave, and the next people would come in--and so on all afternoon.

On other afternoons, Olivia would go to other people's houses and visit them – for, of course, only 15 minutes at each place. The reason for the term calling hours was that people had little white name cards known as "calling cards" to leave as they came in the front hall. They would sit and wait until the servants came out and announced them in. Or, if they couldn't stay, they would just fold down the corner of their cards, put them in the dish, and walk out. That way, Olivia would know that they had stopped by in person. We don't need to be announced, so I'll just close the closet, and lead the way into the drawing room. We can go in either door; it doesn't make any difference.

The Visitor Experience at the Mark Twain House

The Drawing Room

The mirror is original – it came from Sam and Olivia's first home in Buffalo, New York. They lived there for the first year of their marriage. The chandelier is also original; it's the only original light fixture in the house. On the left side of the mantel is a photograph of Mrs. Taft – the woman from the other end of the line – with her husband Dr. Cincinnatus Taft.

On the piano – which is exactly like the original – we have photographs of Sam, his in-laws, and his daughters. I'll point them all out. In the picture of two men together, Sam is the one on the right. That's Mark Twain himself. The other one is Charles Langdon, Olivia's younger brother. She also had an older, adopted sister. We'll see a picture of her upstairs. In back, is Olivia's mother, Olivia Lewis Langdon. She would visit here almost all winter. In the summer, they would go to Elmira, New York, to see her. In front, is Olivia's father, Jervis Langdon. He was a lumber and coal dealer who made a million dollars, then died in 1870. He never knew any of his grandchildren. Neither did Sam's father; Sam was twelve years old when his father died. But both the grandmothers got to know the grandchildren very well. Sam's mother lived in Keokuk, Iowa.

They were…from oldest to youngest: Susy, Jean, and Clara. Susy was the eldest, and favorite of the family, Jean was the baby, and Clara, the second daughter, lived to be 88 years old, and became a piano player, a singer, and a biographer. She wrote five books, including one about Sam.

Over here, we have two representations of Olivia. The bust was done when she was nineteen years old; the photograph was taken when she was 24. Sam and

Olivia had known each other for two years before they were married. They were engaged for one year, and they were married on February 2 of 1870. Olivia was 24 years old, and Sam was 34. Despite the age difference, she called Sam "Youth" – because he had a rather exuberant personality. He called her Livy – unless they were with strangers. Then they would call each other Mrs. Clemens and Mr. Clemens. This seems very formal, but that was the custom in 19^t-century American culture.

They met each other through Charles. In 1867, Sam and Charles were two of the 110 passengers aboard the *Steam Ship Quaker City*, which was traveling around the Mediterranean Sea to Europe, the Middle East and northern Africa. Most of the people on the trip were wealthy American tourists, including Charles. He was 18 years old, had never been away from home, and here he was going out of the country. His father thought that this would be a good experience for him, before he took over the family business. Sam was 32 years old; he had lived away from home for twenty years. He had traveled all over his own country, even to Hawaii, and now was paying his way as a journalist. The articles he wrote about his experiences were later compiled into a book in 1869, called *The Innocents Abroad*.

The other 108 passengers aboard were led by Henry Ward Beecher, of New York City. He was a nationally famous preacher, and the younger brother of Sam's future next-door neighbor, Harriet Beecher Stowe. Henry Ward Beecher was leading his wealthy, New York City church people on the trip. Sam found that in observing them, he collected a lot of material for satire about American society. And Charles found that it was much more fun to spend time with Sam than it was to be with the church people. The two became friends. Inevitably, halfway through the trip, Charles got homesick. When that happened, he invited Sam to his cabin and showed him a portrait of his older sister, Olivia. Sam took one look at it and wanted to marry her, but didn't say that for over a year. He waited to meet Olivia and get to know her and her family a bit better first.

As he got to know them, he found that he liked the Langdons very much, and they liked him...as a family friend. He was rather different from them. So, he took a good long look at all of the differences, to see what he could do to change their minds. Here is what he observed:

1. The Langdons were quiet. Sam was just the opposite; he was very witty, loved to tell jokes, and make people laugh.

2. The Langdons were used to surroundings like these – luxuries, decorations and servants. Sam wasn't, but he didn't mind them.

3. Olivia had gone to college – the first women's college in the country, founded in her hometown in 1855: Elmira College. Sam was self-educated from the time his father died.

When he was twelve years old, Sam had to quit school and work in his older brother Orion's print shop for five years. He became a typesetter, and learned all about reporting and editing. As he learned, his reading and writing skills improved. His older sister Pamela taught piano for a living; she taught Sam how to play. He could play the banjo, and he could sing. After that, while working as a Mississippi River steamboat pilot – in Louisiana – he was able to practice French until he became fluent and literate in the language. However, when he got to Paris several years later, no one understood him when he spoke to them in Cajun French. Still, it was a good experience for his writing career.

Another difference was that the Langdons were from the northeast part of the country. They were abolitionists, and had participated in the Underground Railroad system until it was no longer needed. Sam was from the southwest. He had been in the Confederate army for 2 weeks during the Civil War, before deserting. He found he didn't like the conditions, he didn't agree with the politics, and he didn't want to kill people, so he quit, and went West. That way he couldn't be found and dragged back into service.

And last, but not least, the Langdons went to church on Sundays, and they never swore. Sam loved to swear – especially when he knew he wouldn't be caught – and his mother had raised him with the idea that going to church was a punishment. If Sam had done anything bad, she would make him go to church twice instead of once. She knew he didn't like to go.

With all of these differences in mind, Sam was ready to approach Olivia.

He told her that he would attend church every week, pray daily, and never swear – not even when the Langdons couldn't hear him. She didn't say anything until after they were married. Then she promptly released him from the promise; she realized that Sam would not otherwise have chosen to live this way. She said they would now go to church only every three weeks, and just pray there because, "After all," she added, "if you're not going to get into heaven, I don't want to go either."

They were married for 34 years, and she was his editor the entire time. Of her editing, Sam once said: "Mrs. Clemens has kept a lot of things from getting into print that I would not have known any better than to have published, and that would have given me a reputation I would not have cared to have had."

Her favorite things to do for fun were to read and discuss books with her friends. She and Sam held gatherings for this purpose in this room, one evening per week. At one of these gatherings, Sam brought out *Old Fish* – his favorite brand of cigars, which he imported from his hometown of Hannibal, Missouri. He passed them out to the men at the gathering. They all took one puff, choked, gagged, and left. It was the shortest meeting the group ever had.

At least once or twice a month, Olivia would put on elaborate Victorian dinner parties for famous people whom she and Sam had met, and their friends and business colleagues. These were seven-course meals, usually lasting for two or three hours at a time. They included: soup, salad, fruit, meat, poultry, fish, and dessert courses. Each dish was a work of art, both on the platters and on the individual serving plates. Dessert could be ice cream shaped like angels or flowers or hearts.

The girls would not attend; they would eat with their nanny upstairs and then sit halfway down the stairwell, where they could watch their father in the dining room. They thought he was very funny to watch. Most nights, though, it was just the family in there: daughters, grandmother, parents and butler. I'll lead the way in, and tell you about all of the unconventional things that they did in there.

The Dining Room

The wallpaper in here is a reproduction of the original. It's a Japanese design embossed to look like leather. The original was leather, but we couldn't have that again, so the craftspeople just went over every inch of it by hand, rubbing in the finish, until they got the same effect. Candace Thurber Wheeler was the Associated Artist consulted for this room, with its dark red and dark gold flower pattern. She told Olivia that a dining room should have dark surroundings, so as to divert the visitors' attention away from them and onto the bright, white table.

The centerpiece – called an epergne – was a wedding gift to Sam and Olivia, and was used at their reception. The silverware is all original. If you want to, feel free to step up really close and peer at it. Olivia's name is engraved into each piece: Olivia L. Langdon and variations thereof. And notice that there are two forks, two knives, and two spoons at each setting. Sam was raised with one of each, so Olivia had to give him lessons. He wanted the lessons, so that he would know what the rules were before he started to break them. He sat at this end of the table, in one of the original armchairs, so he could watch the snowflakes falling in the winter, seemingly melting into the embers of the fire.

There's the other split chimney. Around it and the fireplace, we have some more Tiffany tiles. On either side there are closets and, off to the left, that door with the mirror over leads to the butler's pantry and what used to be the kitchen and servants' wing beyond.

Both of the sideboard cabinets are original. The one behind me was carved out of mahogany in Boston, in the Eastlake design, and it and the house were designed to fit together. The other one began as a player piano. Sam bought it when it was a desk, and he and Olivia used it there, as you see it.

Most evenings the family would be alone together. The parents sat at either end of the table, and the grandmother and daughters would sit on either side. Most wealthy American parents left their children with the nanny for every meal, but not Sam and Olivia. Because their son had died, they spent as much time as they could with their remaining children. The daughters only ate with their nanny if there were a dinner party going on. Other than that, the whole family would eat breakfast, lunch, and dinner – every day – all together.

Olivia would wait until the family was finished eating, and then go over a list of every social error Sam had made throughout the meal. The girls thought this was great; they called it "dusting off Papa." She would pick on Sam for: using the wrong silverware; talking too much to one person, but not enough to another; monopolizing the conversation; or walking up and down behind his seat, wildly waving his napkin and still talking too much, telling funny stories.

During dinner parties Sam would have to share the floor with his best friend from Hartford, the Reverend Joseph Twichell. He had a lot of funny stories to tell, too. It was to Twichell's Asylum Hill Congregational Church – still standing today – that the family went every few weeks, as Olivia had decreed at the beginning of her marriage. Sam and Twichell liked to go for long walks together. Once they decided to walk to Boston, just to see if they could do it. They turned back at Chicopee. They decided that they could do it, but that they didn't need to actually walk there to prove it. Usually, they contented themselves with ten-mile round-trip walks to Talcott Mountain so that they could look out over Simsbury, talking politics the whole time.

There was one other person in the room, and Clara said that he was here for every meal. He was the butler, and his name was George Griffin. He was a former slave, and he came here to wash windows in 1874. He stayed seventeen years, the whole time the Clemens family did. George was very much a part of the family, so much so that his room was in the family quarters, not the servants' wing. Although he had his own family and place in town, he still needed his old room in case a party were to last until the middle of the night, or in case Sam were to invite him to stay overnight and play billiards. George's room was therefore located on the third floor, appropriately near the billiard room. George would use his room on Friday nights, when Sam invited his friends to come over and play billiards all night. George was counted among these friends, and could go to bed across the hall when the fun ended.

George would come out of the pantry door with the food, walk around the table serving it, maybe start up the music box in the hall, and then stand behind the screen, laughing at Sam's jokes before the punch lines, whether there was company or not. He knew them all by heart, having heard them over and over. Sam didn't care; he loved a good audience. During the day, George would let people in and out of the house, and direct the other servants.

George made $30 a month, $360 a year – not a lot. To supplement his income, he gambled at speakeasys, and he was very good at it. Saturday nights were gambling nights, and Sunday mornings he would be back here, serving breakfast. Susy disapproved of gambling, and was always trying to get him to quit. George would be ready for her. No matter how he had done the night before, he would come into the dining room looking as depressed as possible. He would keep this up until the last dish had been served. When at last he stepped back from the table, Susy would say: "Oh George, I'm so happy! I can tell that you lost a lot of money last night, you've finally learned your lesson, and are now going to quit gambling." Then George would say: "Oh, yes, Miss Susy, I really learned my lesson this time. I only won $800 last night."

Then she would see that she had been fooled again. George stored the cash he won between the two mattresses of his bed in his room upstairs, and would run up there every so often during the day to make sure that it was all still there. It always was.

On most evenings, when they were alone, everyone – including George – would go into the library after dinner, for the evening's entertainment. So, we will go in there.

The Servants' Hall and Butler's Pantry[*]

The butler's pantry is a small room just off of the dining room, shaped like a quarter of a circle. It contained the formal dinnerware and crystal for formal parties, and many of the items on display in it today reflect that intent, even if they are not all original.

It is a beautiful, wood-paneled room, complete with a small pass-through for the cook to present each dish to the butler. George Griffin would have enjoyed this convenience as he brought dish after dish out to Sam and Olivia and their guests.

The room includes a sink, a speaking tube with a room indicator to tell where a call originated from, and plenty of work space.

Down the hallway from the butler's pantry is the kitchen, a small storage room with a boiler, chef's pantry, the servants' dining hall, and a door that leads outside and down a stairway to the ground.

Opposite that door is a staircase that leads upstairs. Up that staircase were rooms for the cook, the maids – who included the family's life-long maid and seamstress, Katy Leary – and a sewing room that was used by Katy Leary.

The kitchen contains yet another speaking tube, through which Olivia could have checked on meal preparations with the cook, a huge stove with a warming oven at the top, and plenty of workspace.

A narrow work area leads off of the kitchen to the butler's pantry, where the cook could pass dishes through to the butler during a dinner party.

---

[*] This portion of the book was written from a visitor's point of view, as the Butler's Pantry and Servants Wing were restored after my time as a historic interpreter at the Mark Twain House.

The Library

Have a look at the carpet; it's a reproduction of late 19th-century wall-to-wall carpeting. It is made with 27-inch-wide strips sewn together – notice the seams.

The books in here are all period copies of the same titles that the family had when they lived here. Among them is a copy of the autobiography of the Civil War Union General and former U.S. President Ulysses S. Grant. He finished dictating it the day before he died of throat cancer. Mark Twain had it published, enabling Grant to leave the proceeds to his widow and family: $200,000. The shelves and the carvings along the tops of the shelves are all made of walnut. The carvings had to be reproduced from photographs, which we were very lucky to have. The Hartford Public Library rented this first floor for 26 years, and amazingly, stupidly, knocked out the original carvings – but we were able to restore them.

The rest of the woodwork in the house is original: the doors, the panelings, the moldings, and this mantelpiece. his mantel was carved out of oak in Scotland, and bought there by Sam and Olivia, who shipped it home with orders to the architect to install it in their library – which he did after cutting off the top. It was too tall. But the top wasn't wasted. Instead, it was installed over the dining room doorframe: there's the rest of it. Sam didn't care that he had the Mitchell-Innes family coat-of-arms carved into his mantel – as long as he personalized it to read "18 **** 74" in the ovals on either side. Before that was done, it read "18" **** "69" for the manor house that was never completed, so the "74" is a bit darker/harder to read.

This Tiffany brass piece over the fireplace was Olivia's idea. It has a Ralph Waldo Emerson quote, which reads:

"The ornament of a house is the friends who frequent it."

Sam was fond of this saying and of quoting it because there were so many visitors here.

There were lunches, teas, dinners, and parties. There were three guestrooms, one on each floor, all usually occupied; and there was Nook Farm's open-door policy – visitors could arrive at any time, unannounced. Imagine a hundred years ago: this was the edge of Hartford, not the middle. There were just eighteen mansions, some with carriage houses, and only woods and brush in between. Beyond all of this, there were more woods, and the town of West Hartford in the distance.

People felt quite safe in this neighborhood. There was no need to lock their doors, and so they would just wander in and out of each other's homes for casual visits. When she was near the end of her life, and a bit confused, Harriet Beecher Stowe, who maintained a wonderful garden with cocoa mulch outside her own home, liked to go into the conservatory and pick flowers. Olivia told the servants to "let Mrs. Stowe do whatever she liked".

Look in the conservatory: it has been restored to its original appearance. We know that there was a small fountain, a circular walkway, a lot of plants, Japanese lanterns, and an original plant. The plant was grown from a cutting of the ficus – or fig – vine plant that Olivia had when she lived here. She gave it to the family doctor, and his descendants took care of it until the house was restored, and then gave it back. So now we have this responsibility to keep a 121-year-old plant alive. So far, so good.

There are several original items in this room. This is the grandmother's rocking chair. This is the only original painting in the entire house: it's Italian, it's by Ransoni, and the girls called it "Emmeline." The sofa is original, as well as Susy's matching rocking chair, Sam's smoke-stand, his red plush chair, and the carved table from Italy. In the late 1870s (1877 to 1878), the family went traveling for over a year in France, Germany, Austria, Italy, Switzerland, and Greece. They spent a lot of time in Heidelberg, Germany. The family toured, Sam wrote, and Olivia did a lot of shopping for this house.

After dinner, they would all come in here. Olivia and her mother would sit on either side of the fireplace to read and talk while the others played jungle. George would get in the conservatory and growl; he was the tiger. Sam would crawl around on the floor out here with the girls on his back; he was the elephant. After enough suspense had been built up, George would leap out and the girls would scream and yell until story-time, which took place in Sam's chair in the alcove. Susy and Clara had created the story-telling system. It required Sam to tell a different story every night, and always without a moment's preparation. He had to start by incorporating a cat-in-the-ruff picture into it, then work his way across the mantel using every item in order, and ending with Emmeline. If at any time he were to deviate from this system, he would have to start over. He often said that "if the bric-a-bracs on the mantel seemed a bit worn out, it was because they had been through so many adventures." They all had to be violent adventures, full of bloodshed – another requirement. Jean always wanted a tiger in her stories.

Once, a play was performed in here. Olivia organized it to surprise Sam. It was based on his book *The Prince and the Pauper*, which he had dedicated to Susy and Clara. The play was performed in front of the conservatory. The sliding doors were pulled shut, and the shade was pulled down for a backdrop. Sam came back from a business trip and found that he had to play the role of Miles Hendon. Susy was the prince, her best friend Daisy Warner was the pauper, and Clara played the Lady Jane Grey, the prince's cousin. Eighty people attended, sitting in rows of chairs stretching from here to the dining room. Everything was going just fine, until Susy was crowned king, and then, in the middle of her soliloquy, her throne toppled over backward. The whole audience jumped up, startled, but Susy didn't miss a beat – she just kept going, delivering her lines to the ceiling, and that's how it ended.

The Mahogany Guest Suite

This next room is called the Mahogany Guest Suite. It is the most elaborately decorated guest room in the house, because first-time visitors would stay here on the first floor to get their first impressions of the house, and, of course, the family wanted them to be good impressions.

The reason that this is called the Mahogany Guest Suite is that the doors, moldings, panelings, bed, and mirror stand are all made of mahogany wood. The bed and mirror stand are original, and they have tiles imported from England built in. The bed is six feet long. It may seem shorter, but that's just because the pillows are propped up. People thought it was healthy to sleep sitting up in the late 19th century. The architect designed this room with that idea in mind, so that you could wake up in the winter, sitting up, and see two seasons at once: snow out three windows, and plants through the other one, in the conservatory.

The wallpaper is a reproduction of the original pattern; bees collecting pollen and nectar from gold-leafed flowers on a background of honeycomb.

Sam's friend from Boston, William Dean Howells, stayed here often with his wife, Eleanor, and called this place "the royal chamber." As soon as a guest arrived, the luggage would be brought in, that door would be closed for privacy, and the guest would then be presented with a key to the veranda doors – so that she or he could come and go unnoticed by the family. Visitors found their own bath and dressing rooms, and room service, which could be ordered through a speaking tube.

There was one of these speaking tubes in each room, and they all connected to the kitchen. The way the speaking tube system worked was that you had to blow through the hole to set off a whistle at the other end. Meanwhile, in the kitchen, the servant would open the tube at their end. Once you had the servant's attention, you would open your end of the tube and ask for something. A maid or butler would appear with it within a few minutes. The system has been disconnected; there are only a few tubes left now.

Look into the bathroom: it has its original mahogany wood paneling, and two period fixtures exactly like the originals. There's a white marble double sink – Howells and his wife could have brushed their teeth both at once. Up to the middle of the left, above the bathtub, is a hot water shower. This was a new invention that Sam had to have. It was so new that they could only get one shower. Of course, that meant that Sam had to come down here from the bathroom he shared with Olivia to use it, but that was okay. He could still brag that he had one of the first hot water showers in all of Hartford. Also, they did have a toilet behind the door, but we don't. We tried to get one, but we couldn't find a never-before-used, historically correct toilet, so we decided to wait. Hopefully, we'll get one someday. Theirs would have been a reach up and pull the chain kind, with a bowl shaped like an elephant's trunk.

Next, we'll go through two doors, including this one. Would the last person through please shut both, and I'll meet everyone out here (said as I reentered the front hall).

Back in the Front Hall, at the Stairwell

Here we are in the front hall – back where we started. That was our camouflage door. Have a look up; I mentioned that the architect designed churches as well as houses. He added a cathedral-like ceiling and church-like banisters to this one which, like those in churches, are short. This does two things for us: it makes the ceiling seem to be higher up, and it makes life dangerous. Please don't anyone, at any time, step up close to the banisters or, worse yet, lean way over. We wouldn't want anyone to fall, and smash our beautiful light fixture, or get hurt. Feel free to touch the banisters for balance as we go up to Sam and Olivia's room and, if you like the idea, touch something they touched.

Olivia's Sewing Alcove

This was Olivia's alcove: she would read and sew in here, and talk to her daughters. Her original sewing table, with its bell-shaped trap door and revolving compartments, is to the left of the sofa. Please go ahead without me, into Sam and Olivia's room.

The Visitor Experience at the Mark Twain House

Sam and Olivia's Room

Well, this is Sam and Olivia's room, and I'm sure that the bed stands out as a rather prominent feature. It was carved out of walnut in Venice, Italy, and bought there by Sam and Olivia (Sam picked it out) for $200 which, in those days, was a lot. Maids earned $150 in year, plus room and board. Having paid so much, of course Sam wanted his money's worth, so he slept with his head at the foot of the bed. These are the pillow ruffles; Sam slept on that side, and Olivia slept on this one. That way they could better appreciate the carvings. Sam thought it would be absurd to pay a lot for something and then not look at it, so he made sure to look. All of the angels are on posts – they're detachable. The girls were allowed to remove them, and play with them like dolls during the day, but they had to be back at night, so that their father could go to sleep with his bed in one piece. They bathed this one, so it's a lighter color than the others – they wore some of the finish off of it. The girls could bathe and powder the angels, wrap them in blankets and rock them in cradles.

Sam didn't have one of these – a cord running from a gas jet down to a reading lamp – when he lived here in Hartford. He had one in New York City after his wife died, when he found that he liked to read, write, sleep and smoke cigars in bed. It was dangerous to do all this next to a gas lamp, but no there were no explosions. A gas cord would have been that much thicker than the electric one you see here today. We show you this here because the house where he lived in Manhattan is gone, and we want you to see this. There are some famous photographs of Sam in this bed, wearing a long white nightshirt, holding a thick, half-smoked cigar, and being interviewed by many reporters, who surround the bed. Books are strewn over the bed.

The door between the bed and the front window leads to a balcony. Sam thought of using it once, but changed his mind at the last second. And that door next to the bed, in the corner, used to lead to Sam and Olivia's dressing and bath area –also known as the swearing room. Sam would go in there each morning, shut the door all the way, and bathe, shave, dress, and swear a lot – to get it out of his system for the day so that he wouldn't be caught later swearing around children. It worked; he was never caught doing that.

Olivia knew all about this all along, but didn't let Sam know she knew until one Sunday morning in 1880, when he forgot to close the door all the way. As usual, he was the first one out of bed and into the bathroom. He absentmindedly left the door a few inches ajar, and bathing and shaving and muttering swears under his breath. Next, he began to get dressed. He put on a shirt, and couldn't feel the buttons up the back, so he swore loudly and threw the shirt out the window. It was followed by two more shirts, and by more swearing. All three shirts landed in the bushes below, for the churchgoers to admire as they passed by.

Then Sam noticed that the door was...not closed. He quickly finished dressing and came out, trying not to look at Olivia, who was glowering at him in the bed. He put his hand on the balcony doorknob, and he was going to go out there, when he realized that he would just have to come back in. So he decided to face the situation, and get it over with. He turned around and then, to his great surprise, Olivia repeated every swear word he had used. She had never sworn before in her entire life. Sam gaped at her in amazement, and then he said: "You've got the words right, Livy, but you don't know the tune." They laughed uproariously, until all was forgiven. Then Olivia got dressed, and they went down to breakfast.

On the bureau is a photograph of Olivia's older adopted sister. She and her husband Theodore lived at Quarry Farm in Elmira, New York, on the edge of town and up a hill a bit – rather isolated from the rest of the town. The Clemens family went to stay with them every summer, for three to six months of the year, and share household expenses. That was where Sam got most of his writing done.

He tried to write here, in Hartford, and he got some work done, but not enough to make a living. Friends, business contacts and, as his fame grew and grew, fans kept interrupting his work. He had to be polite and say something, if only hello to them, but it really cut into his writing time. So he would be rather worried when he got to Quarry Farm.

Mrs. Crane anticipated the problem early on and had a study built – out of earshot of her house – to surprise Sam. It looked like a Mississippi River steamboat pilothouse, with eight sides, windows all around, a peaked roof, a fireplace, ivy growing up all over it, cats who visited and sat with him, and a view of the Chemung River valley. It took Sam right back to the Mississippi River days that he was writing about. The fact that it was out of earshot of her house was its most important feature; Sam was always very easily distracted by sounds from outside. He worked there each day from ten in the morning to five at night without lunch, because he didn't want it.

The only unannounced visitors allowed were cats; humans had to have appointments. He dropped his papers on the floor while he worked. At the end of the day, he would pick them up and go home, and read what he had after dinner by the fire. So, his family heard his works in their original forms, before the editing was done.

Suzy's Room

But Sam wasn't the only author in the family. Susy and Clara each wrote biographies of him. Clara wrote *My Father, Mark Twain* in 1931, when she was fifty-seven years old, and she had the book published. She intended for the world to see what she wrote. Susy, at the age of thirteen, intended no such thing. She kept her work hidden in her room. Olivia found it, showed to Sam, and then they put it back.

Susy wrote *Papa*, a series of journal entries about Sam, when she was thirteen years old. She wrote for about a year, for fun, then stopped. She hid the manuscript in her room. She knew that her parents knew she was writing. Many years later, Sam found her work again, read it, wrote lots of stories about Susy and the family, and shuffled them in among her journal entries. Then he put it all aside. And then, in 1985, a hundred years after the work was begun, Charles Neider found it, read it, and published it under Susy's title *Papa*.

Today, both books are available for anyone in the world to see, in libraries and in second-hand bookshops. They have gone out of print, most annoyingly.

Have a look across the alcove into Susy's room – I'll meet you there and tell you where she hid the book.

It was the custom in wealthy families for the oldest child to have her own room, and for the other children to share until they grew up. Then they all got their own rooms. It was under the bed in here that Olivia found the biography of Sam. She showed it to him, and he was thrilled, so after that, whenever he said something witty, Susy knew that "that was for the biography."

By 20th and 21st century standards, this is a typical teenager's room – but not by 19th century standards. There are lots of things pinned up, randomly, on the walls, especially over the desk on the right. Susy was ahead of her time, doing something that teenagers commonly do today, and this was because of her father. Sam had to go on many business trips to Boston and New York City. Whenever he was away, there would be constant letters back and forth between Sam and Olivia, and Sam and the girls. One time, while he was in New York, staying in the home of his friend Thomas Nast – the famous cartoonist – he was walking around on the second floor of the house. He noticed that the oldest daughter had decorated her room like this, and he wrote home suggesting that Susy might want to do the same thing. She did; Sam was a very attentive father.

Outside Katy Leary's Sewing Room

There's a closed door out here – it led to Katy Leary's sewing room. [Today, it leads to a curator's office.] Like Olivia, she was from Elmira. She was hired there in the summer of 1880, when she was seventeen years old, to be Olivia's private maid and the family seamstress. Katy made all of Olivia's dresses, complex projects which displayed the latest fashions. She worked with the family for thirty years, met famous people, and traveled to Europe. She quit when Sam died. Then she went home to Elmira, ran a boarding house, and wrote a book about her life with the Clemens family.

The Grandmother's Room

This was the second-floor guestroom – the grandmother's room. In it is Herter Brothers' furniture with Chinese embroidered silk. It was Sam's idea to set this room aside for Olivia Lewis Langdon, because she was here so long and often. They got along well, and exchanged a lot of letters. He once wrote to her, "the sooner you get here...the satisfactorier." He liked to make up words.

She must have realized that he was teasing her when he wrote his list of *Things to Do In Case of Fire*. Number 27 was "Save your mother-in-law." There were only twenty-seven things on the list. A lot higher up on it was "Save your wife and cat."

Sam loved cats; he had eleven, including Satan and Sin, a mother cat and kitten who lived close to the inferno of the coal furnace in the cellar. Other cats' names were Stray Kit, Sour Mash, Soapy Sal, Buffalo Bill, Pestilence, Famine, Lazy, Frauline, and Apollinaris.

The girls named the four dogs: I Know, You Know, Don't Know, and Hash. The Know dogs were collies, all acquired at once. Hash was a mutt. He was a big dog, with floppy brown or black ears and some spots.

The Visitor Experience at the Mark Twain House

The School Room

The girls had a schoolroom here. They studied at home. They could eat popcorn while they worked, and they could have their pets in and out of the room. We'll go in that room next.

This is the schoolroom, and that basket on a stick, next to the fireplace, is a popcorn popper. The girls would have used something like that. They didn't just study in here; they had games, toys, fans that their father bought in Hawaii (on an 1866 business trip), and dresses that their mother didn't want anymore. We have a few period dresses laid out here as examples. The girls liked to have the skirts trailing behind them as they played Queens at war with one another: Mary, Queen of Scots and Queen Elizabeth the First of England. Jean would sit at her desk and write death warrants for the older girls, and fall asleep when she wasn't writing. The parents liked to watch these proceedings – surreptitiously.

But about the work: Olivia taught the girls herself here, hired tutors for them, and a German nanny who wasn't allowed to speak English around them. Only German, so that they would be well prepared when they went to Germany and Austria. Later on, the girls also learned to speak French fluently.

The girls followed a very strict routine: in the mornings, they were taught geography, history, English literature, math, science, German, French, Polish, Russian, and Greek. In the afternoons they would work on their assignments, and then they could play.

When the girls finished studying here, they attended Hartford Public High School, and did well. Susy later attended Bryn Mawr College, in Pennsylvania, for about a year. And then, in the

1890s, the family was in Europe. Clara spent some time studying piano playing and singing at boarding schools there. She began her work for her career in this room.

When she was six years old, Clara received a piano for Christmas – exactly like this one. When she grew up, she met Ossip Gabrilowitsch, a Russian pianist and conductor who lived in Vienna, Austria. They knew each other for over ten years before they were married. When they first met, Clara told Ossip that she had no intention of ever getting married. He told her that he hoped to marry her someday. It took him more than a decade, but he convinced her to marry him. She had just been worried that if she got married, she wouldn't be able to have a career, but she had one.

Clara and Ossip's wedding was performed by none other than the Reverend Joseph Twichell. Clara talked about Twichell in her memoirs about Sam. It seemed that he and Twichell liked to chat outside the church, after his sermons, and Sam said one day, "You know Joe, that's a clever trick you have, of pounding the pulpit extra hard, when you haven't got anything to say." He replied, "It was equally clever of you to have discovered it, Sam."

Anyway, he did Clara's wedding, with no obey clause, as she requested, on October 6 of 1909. At Clara's request, Sam wore his white suit, which he called his "don'tcareadamns," and his cap and gown from Oxford University. She and Ossip were quite happy until he died in 1936. They had one daughter. Her name was Nina – she became a musician, though not famous, and did not get married or have any children. Neither did Susy or Jean, so this family has no direct descendents. They are all buried at Woodlawn Cemetery in Elmira, New York, with the

The Visitor Experience at the Mark Twain House

Langdons of their generation, and Sam's grave is a Twain high with a fathom Marker – for Mark Twain. Clara had it put up the year after Ossip died, to honor both Sam and Ossip.

But, to make sure that you won't think that there is no one alive now with any connection to the family who lived here, I must tell you that there are many descendents of both extended families alive today. The Clemenses have moved to southern California, and the Langdons still live in Elmira, New York, and spend their summers at Quarry Farm. Except for the youngest, who lives in Virginia – he's in the military.

Clara and Jean's Room

Next, we'll see Clara and Jean's room – the nursery. The toys are all period pieces, similar to the ones that the girls played with, except for one detail: the girls had more toys. Sam was always bringing some home from his business trips, to surprise his daughters. He hated to go away, and when he had to, he and Olivia, and he and his daughters would send letters back and forth to each other, constantly.

The wallpaper is a reproduction of the original; it's Walter Crane's English nursery rhyme theme *Ye Frog He Would A-Wooing Go*. There are two versions to this story – one of them is depressing, so I won't tell you that one yet. In the cheerful version, a frog went a-courting, to convince a mouse to marry him. She agreed to it, a rat was the preacher at the wedding. After the ceremony, they had a party with the rat. Then everyday life began. The frog played the violin, the mouse supported them by spinning, and they stayed friends with the rat. They were also friends with a cat, her kittens, and a duck. They lived happily ever after. The end.

That was the cheerful version. Here's the other one: a frog went to visit a mouse. On the way there, a rat joined him. When they arrived, they found her spinning. She stopped and invited them to have a tea party with her. Just as they were sitting down to enjoy the food, a cat and her kittens burst in and ate the rat and the mouse. The frog ran off in a panic, and a duck ate him. The end.

This is the nursery bathroom. It has period, child-size fixtures: a commode, sink and tub. The Clemens girls all shared this room.

About the beds – the brass bed is a period piece, and it would have been for Clara. The crib was for

Jean. The crib is original; all the Clemens girls used it. And, on the wall between the two, is another speaking tube. It would have been used to call for breakfast, and to talk to Santa Claus at Christmastime. This was before going to the mall to see Santa – before malls were invented. Clara would have asked for her piano through this tube.

She was the most accident-prone member of the entire family, even though she lived the longest, to be eighty-eight years old. Throughout her life, she was always having accidents, and always recovering without a scratch. Her mother once commented, "It's amazing, how Clara always seems to escape with her life." And her father replied, "Yes, I suppose God doesn't care very much about meeting her." When she had the mumps, the girls were put to bed, the humidifier was set up, and the nanny left the room for only a moment, but that was all that was necessary. She came back to find Clara sleeping soundly – with all of her quilts on fire. She must have thrashed around a bit too close to the humidifier. The nanny yanked Clara out of bed and threw the quilts out the window, in the snow, burning her hands in the process. Clara grew up completely unscathed. This was typical of an accident involving Clara

We'll go upstairs now, but as we go, please be careful of the low banisters. We think Clara may have fallen over them at one point. She was fine; it was her parents who got so upset.

The Third Floor

This is the third floor landing, which the architect designed to look like a church. That's an original Clemens seat like a church pew, facing an alcove with an archway like a pulpit. Then we have the cathedral-like ceiling, and clearstory windows. If the family had wanted to, they could have stayed home on Sundays and hired a preacher. But they didn't want to.

The doors all lead to the Billiard Room, the alcove, the Texas-deck, a closet, another closet, George Griffin's room, and what used to be the bathroom. The connecting doors inside of it are still there. The butler and the guests would not have had to go into the hall to use the bathroom.

Look into George Griffin's room. It was restored in 1998. Everything is as it was when he used it, except one thing: no money. He kept the cash from his speakeasy winnings stuffed under the mattress, and would run upstairs several times a day to make sure that it was all still there. Of course it was – no one took his money. On Friday evenings, from shortly after dinner until far into the night, Sam would play billiards with his friends – who included George Griffin. He would go to bed across the hall from the Billiards Room when the guests left.

That thing up there is an annunciator. It's an intercom indicator, and has nothing to do with the Clemens family. It is an electrical device that was installed by the subsequent owners of the house in 1903.

This room can be referred to in three ways: it can be the third-floor guestroom; or the Artist's Friends' Room; or the second-time visitor's room. Second-time visitors would stay here for their second

The Visitor Experience at the Mark Twain House

impressions of the house. This was the policy; first time visitors got their first impressions in the Mahogany Room, second time visitors got their second impressions in this room, and it didn't matter where third time visitors stayed – by then, they would have seen the whole place. Mr. Cable stayed here, when he didn't have mumps, and received his second impression of the house.

Clara wrote about the events leading up to her alleged fall in her memoirs. She said that when she and Susy were under ten years old, they used to feed the squirrels in secret, out the door to the Texas deck. Their parents put an end to this, and told the girls to stay off the third floor until they were older. So, they convinced themselves that they didn't want to come up here. They believed that a pirate lived in that closet, and that the ghost from Charlotte Bronte's novel *Jane Eyre* lived in the guest room. Sam did nothing to discourage these beliefs.

This portrait of Sam was painted when he was fifty years old, by Dora Wheeler Keith. She was a very talented daughter of one of the Associated Artists who was here at Nook Farm for fifteen months, painting the other famous people. She came to Sam last, and did his portrait under protest. He sat for it under protest; they didn't like each other. They got along with other people, just not each other.

He's sitting in a red chair, because he knew she didn't like red. He has one of his corncob pipes, because he knew she disapproved of smoking. When he wasn't smoking those, he smoked long, thick cigars. But he didn't think that he smoked too many, because he smoked only one at a time. The book is Robert Browning's poetry. She was heard to remark that she didn't like it. That reminded Sam that he did, so he read to her from it while she worked. Other than that, I assure you that Sam was a nice guy. Once a week, he would memorize some of that poetry to recite to his wife and her friends. They liked it. Then they would all talk about it – again, Olivia's favorite pastime. Next, we'll see the Billiards Room, where Sam wrote, and played.

The Billiards Room

Have a look directly up: notice the billiard game pieces stenciled in the middle of the ceiling and, in the corners, crossed pipes and cigar barrels. At the far end of the room, in white marble windows, those themes are repeated. They read "18" and "74," for the year the family moved in, with a "C" for Clemens in each one. The windows and stencilings were gifts from Edward Tuckerman Potter, the architect. The house came with them.

This mahogany billiards table was a gift from a friend – a replacement. Sam had worn his other table out by always playing until three in the morning or dawn and never getting tired, either of being up, or of playing. Then he'd show up the next morning, at 8 a.m., on time for breakfast and fully awake, telling jokes to his daughters, one of whom did this crayon picture. We don't know which one. We also don't know the identity of the amateur Nook Farm artist was who did this color-by-numbers portrait of him.

In the afternoons, Olivia would sit by "18-and-billiards" and edit Sam's work. She was proofreading, and deleting profanity and slightly wild, outrageous stories, which he knew had to come out, but he put them in on purpose, because he knew that his daughters enjoyed hearing them each evening by the fire.

As soon as they were finished laughing, their mother would reach out and fold down the corners of the pages they were on – to mark them for later. They said that it always meant that "some wonderfully fascinating passage must be struck from the book." Later, they understood her point of view. The proofreading was fine, but the profanity Sam wanted to keep, so he tried balancing it out with Bible quotes in *Tom Sawyer*. It didn't work – Olivia just changed "hell" to "thunder" throughout.

That's Sam's Bible back there on the chest, and above it, on the wall, is a copy from the original illustration series of *The Adventures of Tom Sawyer*, by John George Brown.

Sam kept his desk facing away from the windows because, as he explained to Clara, he found squirrels and pigeons 'absolutely fascinating." That often meant that he'd have to pull down some of the shades, as he couldn't turn his back on all of the windows.

But George Griffin was the toughest distraction to ignore. George had to announce the ever-visiting, unwanted visitors. The problem was that Olivia had forbidden both Sam and George to lie, and she was usually sitting right there, editing, so they couldn't conceal a thing. So George would come up here and say, "Mr. Clemens, I left Mr. Joe Schmoe waiting downstairs to see you." Olivia had forbidden Sam to lie, and he didn't want to visit, so after a while he picked up on the loophole that George left and developed an alternative plan. He would go out one of these doors – to the Texas-deck, the balcony or the porch, which was his favorite – and stand there and call to George, "Tell him I've just stepped out." Because this was technically true, Sam was off the hook.

Still, both inventing and using the scheme was rather time-consuming, so it meant that Sam had just that much less time to work on *The Adventures of Tom Sawyer, The Adventures of Huckleberry Finn, Life on the Mississippi, A Tramp Abroad, Roughing It, The Prince and The Pauper*, and *A Connecticut Yankee in King Arthur's Court* here, and he'd have to finish them in Elmira. But he could write short stories here, and get those done.

The Visitor Experience at the Mark Twain House

One of them was called *Taming the Bicycle*, about a penny-farthing model bike that he bought in Hartford. It came with eight one-and-a-half hour lessons, all taught by an Expert, which was spelled with a capital "E". Sam's Expert didn't know what he was getting himself in for; Sam kept falling on the Expert with the bike on top of the two of them, and he wrote that an Expert made an excellent shock absorber. Sam went to visit the Expert in the hospital. When he was released, the Expert brought an army of four more Experts to complete the contract. At last, on his own, Sam hit every rock and dog he encountered. But he still enjoyed the experience; he concluded it with: "Get a bicycle; you will not regret it, if you live."

The family was happy here for seventeen years, and then they left. The reason was that Sam had invested too much money in the Paige typesetter – that huge machine you saw as you bought your tickets for the tour. It's about as long and wide as this table, and about this high. It was maybe the fourth or fifth fastest thing to today's word processor, setting 300 words a minute, and breaking every five minutes. It never worked. Mr. Paige was very persuasive; for fifteen years the inventor kept telling Sam that with just a few more dollars and few more adjustments, he could make it work. $200,000 later, Sam didn't think so. To say the very least, that was more than Olivia had paid for her house, carriage house, land, renovations, decorations, furnishings and bric-a-bracs. She had paid a total of $131,000 and gotten a lot more for her money.

Well, Sam was very honest, determined to pay back every penny, and after eight years (1891-1899) of lecturing around the world and living as cheaply as he could while he traveled with his family, the whole debt was paid. Then he went on to make a lot more money from future writings and lectures, so it was only a temporary financial setback.

And Sam had learned his lesson about investments. He still made them, but after the Paige fiasco, he would pull out of anything that wasn't going well – in other words, all invention investments – early, before he was very heavily in debt.

The family traveled to France, Germany, Austria, Italy, Switzerland, Greece, Russia, California, Vancouver, Hawaii, Australia, New Zealand, Sri Lanka, India, South Africa, then up to London, England, Paris, France, and Vienna, Austria again. And then the debt was paid.

Clara enjoyed traveling very much, especially to restaurants in Europe, because people would invariably point from across the room, and say, "There's Mark Twain!" "There's Mark Twain!" One day, someone said it, and Sam said: "There's Oscar Wilde!" and they rushed up to meet each other, having never met before. She loved to watch things like this.

In India, it was hot. Sam was 60 years old, and his hair, eyebrows and mustache had all turned completely white. As usual, he wanted to be unique, so he decided to adopt a custom of Indian men – wearing all white. He had a lot of white suits made up, and he told Clara that from now on, he would just wear white. If he were going on a visit, he would say, "Dear Madam, may I come in my don'tcareadamns?" ...and then wear the suit no matter what she said.

That was the fun part of their travels. But, there was a downside to all of this – it began in 1889, when Theodore Crane died of a stroke. He and Sam had been good friends every summer at Quarry Farm.

In 1890, both of the grandmothers died. Sam's mother was 88 years old; Olivia's was 80. Olivia happened to be sick at the time, so they missed the funerals.

In 1895, while they were traveling, Jean was diagnosed with epilepsy.

She was 15 years old, and there were no effective treatments for it. Well, there were treatments – they just weren't effective. She lived another fourteen years.

Then there was a thirteen-month separation for the family – July 1895 to August 1896. Clara went with her parents around the world, from California to London. When they got to London, they rented a house and waited for the others to join them.

The others, Katy Leary, Susy, and Jean, had stayed all year at Quarry Farm with their aunt Susan. On the way to meet the boat to go to London, they stopped off here at Nook Farm, but not at this house. It was closed up. Instead, they stayed with Susy's best friend, Daisy Warner. They had a nice visit, but on the day that they were to leave, Susy got sick. She asked that the home she had grown up in be opened up for her. It was, and she was taken to her parents' room on the second floor. Katy Leary nursed her there, round the clock, for three days straight. Halfway through that time, the doctor knew what was wrong. Susy had spinal meningitis. She died on August 18, 1896, at 7:07 p.m. She was 24 years old.

Clara and Olivia had boarded a steamboat for America as soon as they received the telegram about Susy's illness. The rides took two weeks. They simply followed the coffin out to Elmira. Sam got the news alone in London, by telegram. He came right home to his house, just to be in it one last time.

Olivia didn't want any strangers in her home after

that; she had previously hired a husband and wife – gardeners by the names of John and Ellen O'Neill – to look after the place.

At this point, she rented it out for two years, to her college friend Alice Hooker Day. Her family simply moved in with bare essentials; everything belonging to the Clemens family was left intact, such as furnishings and decorations.

A daughter in the family, Katherine Seymour Day, was here for six months, and she got to know the place very well. Then she left; she went traveling and studying around the world for thirty years. She returned to Nook Farm in 1927, bought her great-aunt Harriet Beecher Stowe's house, and lived there until her death at the age of 94 in 1964.

She saved the other four original buildings, which you see here today, while she lived here. So, we have Katherine Seymour Day to thank for making today's visit possible. But, to return to the story....

In 1897, George Griffin died [at the age of 48] of a heart attack while living on his own in New York City. Clara found out, and wrote that it felt as if a member of her family had passed away. There seemed to be nothing to return to here in Hartford. The family moved to New York City when the lecture tour was over. Later, they bought a house in Riverdale, New York, a suburb.

After Life in the Hartford House

This house was put on the market in 1902, and it sold the following year for $27,000. The value of Victorian homes had plummeted at the turn of the century.

In 1903, Olivia's health was failing. She required constant care by Clara and her doctors, who recommended a warm winter in Florence, Italy. Olivia had enjoyed Florence very much on previous visits; the family rented a villa there in early 1904. The move did not improve her health and she died on June 5 of 1904, at 9:15 at night. She was 58 and a half years old. She had always wanted to die before Sam, so she had her wish, but poor Sam was left a widower for the last six years of his life. He wrote to all of his friends "I wish I were with Livy." At her funeral in Elmira, New York, he vowed never again to attend another family funeral.

He moved back to New York City while he had his last home built, in Redding, Connecticut. Clara oversaw its construction and named it *Stormfield*, for one of his short stories: *Extract from Captain Stormfield's Visit to Heaven*. That one had helped to pay for the new place.

That same year, 1907, Oxford University of England invited Sam to receive an honorary doctorate. Yale would later on do the same thing. This was quite a thrill for a man with no degrees, not even one from junior high school. His daughters worried about him, traveling alone, but he did fine, and returned having added a red and blue cap and gown to his don'tcareadamns. So there he was, in red, white, and blue.

Sam loved to dress up in bright colors and now had the perfect excuse.

He did this whenever possible, and even wore the combination to Clara's wedding, at her request. It was held at Stormfield.

After the wedding, Clara and Ossip moved to Vienna, Sam studied astronomy, and Jean was having a nice time preparing for Christmas until Christmas Eve morning, when Katy Leary found her. She was 29 years old, and she had died of heart failure, during an epileptic seizure. Jean was buried in Elmira two days after Christmas. Katy Leary took care of all funeral and burial arrangements and then returned to Stormfield. Sam kept his word about not attending another family funeral. He sent Clara and Ossip a telegram, telling them not to come home for it.

In early 1910 Sam said, "I came into this world with Halley's Comet, and it shall be the greatest disappointment of my life if I don't go out with it, as I expect to." He was born on November 30, 1835. His mother saw the comet in the sky that night. He lived on a few more months, and then died the perfect death. The comet was seen the evening before he died. Sam died on April 21st of 1910, at 6:32 at night, at Stormfield, in his angel bed, with Clara and Ossip by his side. Just before he died, he looked at Clara and saw that she was pregnant, then died at the age of 74 and a half of heart failure, due to too much smoking, and to depression. He had missed Olivia.

But that's too grim a note on which to conclude the tour, so I won't end it that way. Instead, I'll tell you what Sam wrote about this house after Susy died. He took a last look, got his angel bed, and then he went out. And in 1896 he wrote:

"To us, our house was not unsentient matter – it had a heart,

and a soul, and eyes to see us with; it was of us, and we were

in its confidence, and lived in its grace and in the peace of

its benediction. We never came home from an absence that its

face did not light up and speak out its eloquent welcome, and

we could not enter it unmoved."

So, they still thought of this place as a cheerful one, full of good memories. As soon as they had a bad one, they left. They wanted to remember this only as the house where the daughters grew up, where Olivia enjoyed editing and seeing her friends, and where Sam lived when he became world-famous. So please think of this house only in those cheerful, happy terms, as the family chose to. Thank you very much for coming.

Part Two:
The Making of a Historic Interpreter

Training

At the Mark Twain House, tour guides are given a special and, perhaps, pretentious-sounding title: **Historic Interpreter**. In common everyday usage, however, we are referred to as guides, both by ourselves and by others. The purpose of the exalted title of historic interpreter is to distinguish us from volunteers. At many other museums, the term "tour guide" is used to refer to an unpaid worker who prevents visitors from getting lost, and who can point out some exhibits…without going into great detail.

Historic interpreters at the Mark Twain House have a unique program of training to complete before going out in the proverbial field. It never ceases to amaze me when visitors to the house comment on the amount of information conveyed by the guides. They always say that no other historic house museum that they have been to offered such an extensive, in-depth coverage of the given subject matter.

A significant factor in this equation is the selection process which prospective guides must undergo. The Director of Education looks for people with backgrounds in history, art history, literature, historic preservation, theater arts, teaching, and so on. Candidates of all ages, from eighteen and up, are accepted for the job. A guide can be a college student or a retired schoolteacher, a lawyer, a special agent from the Federal Bureau of Investigation, an author, or even a professional tour guide with a one-person owned and operated tour bus, incorporated. One need only have an interest in museums and in Mark Twain, some skill at assembling a captivating presentation, and an aptitude for public speaking.

Once a person has been selected to become a guide, she or he is given a reading list, and a week to complete it. The list consists of several books, some to be read in their entirety, and some of which only specific sections must be read. Also during that week, the trainee is instructed to accompany two or three seasoned guides on their tours. The purpose of this is to see how a tour is done. Trainees are given these opportunities in order that they may see the freedom of expression that the guides enjoy; each guide has a different speaking style and delivery of jokes and anecdotes. Trainees will notice these seasoned guides following proper traffic procedures within the house, i.e. who is to go where and at what point in the tour. And, trainees will notice methods of artifact protection, both polite, calm ones, and more urgent ones, depending on what happens during each tour observed. After each tour, the trainee will have the opportunity to ask the seasoned guide questions like: "What should I do if a situation such as _____ arises?" and to verify any facts about Mark Twain and history, etc. that seem necessary. In addition to all of this, the trainee is sent into the house alone, carrying only a pencil (no pens allowed!) and a pad of paper. The trainee is expected to walk through the house – avoiding tours as much as possible – writing a list of the original artifacts that she or he wishes to discuss on tours.

At the end of the week, the trainee is tested by the Director of Education. It is not the scary experience of taking a test in school; the Director is very nice, and will talk to the trainee for about forty-five minutes as they walk through the house together. Through this long conversation about people, events, artifacts, rules, and procedures, she gets a sense of what the trainee now knows. Then the test is over. If the trainee passes, she or he is then pronounced an historic interpreter – and is sent out into the field to do tours. If not, the trainee is then retrained for another week. But I have never heard of a case in which someone did not pass.

Once a trainee graduates to the level of historic interpreter, she or he must do tours with no further preparation. There is more than one reason for this, not the least of which is to force new guides out into the public's view as quickly as possible, before stage fright has a chance to set in. Providing an interpreter with immediate exposure to public speaking is the quickest way to prevent stage fright. This precludes inexperience from provoking speculation about what the audience might be thinking about how and what a guide is saying. The sooner a guide proves to herself or himself that she or he can handle addressing groups of up to eighteen people, the better. The second and third tours done by that guide will be easier and easier, until speaking feels like a part of daily routine. This can do great things for a person's self-confidence.

Another reason for sending a new guide out without further preamble is that the Mark Twain House has a wonderful policy: no canned tours. This means that each guide is free to create her or his own tour, through point of view, speaking style, choice of anecdotes, area of interest (i.e., family history, art history, literature, etc.), and their individual personalities. Specific facts must be presented by everyone, however, such as why Mark Twain moved to Hartford, who decorated the house, and who lived and worked in it. The guides do not, as a rule, write their tours down – especially in the beginning. Each guide is told to go out and "wing it" – to simply talk to a group of visitors about what she or he knows. After a while, a pattern usually develops in the guide's lectures. Some guides like to talk about something different each time they lead people through the house. Others like to talk about everything they know. Either way, each guide is doing something different from the others. That is why visitors do not get bored with our tours. The philosophy at the Mark Twain House is that in order to generate a continued interest in our presentations, we must maintain variety. Mark Twain would have approved – he wrote a scathing review of a canned tour guide presentation in his first book, *The Innocents Abroad*.

Even after the formal period of training, it can truthfully be said that no historic interpreter's education is ever finished. Guide training goes on for as long as an interpreter works in the house. Here are some of the fun and fascinating things that we do in the morning, early in the evening, on weekends, and at lunchtime:

We meet the curator in the house. She tells us about various original artifacts in each room, and we ask about others. We write down everything that she talks about. This keeps us current on any changes or additions to the museum's collection.

We follow the education director through the house. She tells us about all of the paintings, giving artists' names, titles of the paintings, and some background on each. We ask questions, and write it all down.

We bring our notebooks to the carriage house – which is a beautiful lecture hall inside – and listen to the assistants to the curator and the education director talk about their latest research. One particularly relevant topic was that of the Clemens family butler, George Griffin. The assistant curator told us how old he was when he worked in the house, how much he was paid, his time as a slave, and some details about his family.

We attend symposia, which can be all day or even multi-day affairs. Four lectures per day, two before and two after lunch, are standard program fare. If we find a topic to be of special interest, we ask the bosses to sign us up in advance – before the allotment of guides tickets is filled, and after all guides needed to give tours at that time are scheduled to do so. Topics range from art to politics, literature to comedy, history to art history, etc. There is plenty of variety. Some memorable symposia have covered book banning, the Tiffany Company's stained glass, racism in literature, and Victorian art and architecture. Guest speakers come from colleges and universities all over the country, as well as from newspapers and Hollywood. Hal Holbrook, the consummate Mark Twain impersonator, came to tell about his lifetime of experiences playing and interpreting Mark Twain.

We learn new interpretation techniques as the Director of Education creates them. These include, but are not limited to, theme tours and child-oriented tours, shortened tours, and specialty tours, which focus on a particular area of interest, such as the paintings or furnishings in the house.

We were admitted to free, private showings of new movies based on books by Mark Twain, such as *The Adventures of Huck Finn*.

And, once in a while, a lucky few of us enjoyed the privilege of going on field trips to other historic sites where Mark Twain spent his time. One of these was to the town of his in-laws, the Langdons: Elmira, New York.

Field Trip to Elmira, New York

On Mother's Day of 1992, eight of us went on this trip, including the Visitor Center Administrator, her assistant, five full-time historic interpreters, and Ernest Shaw, owner and operator of Heritage Trails, his one-bus tour company. Our transportation was his bus, and he was our driver. We met him at six o'clock in the morning at one place, and rode with him to another place to pick up the others at 6:30 a.m. Then we were off, driving on the highways of Upstate New York for several hours – plus pit stops and meal stops.

We arrived at 1 p.m., checked into the Mark Twain Motor Inn, and headed for Elmira College. Elmira College, the first women's college in the United States, was founded in 1855 by several wealthy people in that town, including Mark Twain's father-in-law, Jervis Langdon. There, we met Gretchen, who showed us the college's three museum rooms. These rooms featured a Langdon family cradle, a Langdon bed, Mark Twain's typewriter, other artifacts too numerous to name, and lots and lots of photographs and portraits of Langdons, Clemenses, and Beechers. The Reverend Thomas Kennicot Beecher (younger brother of Harriet Beecher Stowe) lived in Elmira, and he officiated at the February 2, 1870 wedding of Samuel Langhorne Clemens (a.k.a. Mark Twain) and Olivia Louise Langdon – along with the Reverend Joseph Twichell of Hartford, Connecticut.

Next, we were shown Mark Twain's study, inside and out. It has been moved from its original site to the Elmira College campus by Langdon family descendants. The study has eight sides, windows all around, a fireplace, and a peaked roof. Ivy used to grow all over it, and Mark Twain would stay in it all day, almost every day of the summer for seventeen years. It is now open to the public in the summer. The study was built as a surprise for Twain by his wife's older sister, Susan Langdon Crane, who lived with her husband Theodore at Quarry Farm, up a hill on the edge of town. The study, on its original site, commanded a view of the town and of the Chemung River Valley. (The river has since been buried.)

After that, Gretchen took us to the edge of town and up a hill to Quarry Farm, pointing out some things along the way. On the left, as we drove up the hill, she indicated two crumbling stone posts, with nothing but a wooded area beyond. This had been the site of the Elmira Watercure Resort. Dr. Rachel Gleason and her husband – also a doctor – practiced a sectarian form of medicine there known as hydropathy. In other words, they prescribed and provided daily baths of all kinds for their patients: sitz baths, shower baths, baths for various parts of the body, etc. They also prescribed daily strolls around a pond that has ceased to exist, and a healthy diet of three balanced meals a day. The most remarkable aspect of the watercure is the practice of bathing daily. To many people in the nineteenth century, this was much more of a luxury than a daily routine for maintaining health. Dr. Rachel Gleason is remembered by Twain historians for helping his wife, Olivia – in her parents' house in town – to give birth to her oldest daughter, Susy.

On the right, Gretchen pointed out the house that used to belong to the Reverend Thomas Kennicot Beecher and his wife, Julia. The house has been considerably updated, with many late twentieth century home improvements – it is well maintained, but not as a museum. A young family lives there now. The Reverend Beecher was an unconventional person – but that was par for the course if one happened to be a member of the Beecher family. He would wear old clothes during the week, and walk around town repairing things for widows, older residents, and anyone else who needed help with home maintenance. He played games and would, once in a while, stop at Klapproth's Saloon for a beer. On weekends, he would get dressed up and preach. He had no trouble gathering an audience; if Beecher found that he could not seat everyone in his church, he would hold services at the Elmira Opera House. It seemed logical to him, but shocked his clerical counterparts. Later on, his congregation built the Park Street Church for him. His wife Julia was his equal partner both in church and in her disdain for convention. She taught Sunday school, and wore her hair short – just down to her shoulders. They had no children.

Just as Thomas and Julia Beecher's home was pointed out, Gretchen turned left, and told us to look to her left. We did, and saw the hill leading up to Quarry Farm. Quarry Farm belonged to Olivia Clemens' older adopted sister, Susan Langdon Crane – Mark Twain's sister-in-law. She lived here with her husband, Theodore and, during the summer, her sister's entire family. The farm has a wonderful view of Elmira. Mark Twain's study was up past the yard at the left front of the house, so he enjoyed this view as he wrote his famous novels. As for the house, it is large and comfortable, and has some beautiful green tiles around the fireplace in its front room. The tiles depict some frogs at play, and the Clemens girls created a story-telling system for their father using those frogs. (Each evening, both in Hartford and in Elmira, Mark Twain was required to tell stories to his daughters that incorporated objects around him. The objects were of his daughters' choosing, and the stories had to be completely spontaneous.)

The first thing I noticed, however, was that directly under a huge photograph of Sam smoking a cigar, someone had placed a sign: "Thank you for not smoking." The next room had one thousand, six hundred books in it. We were not shown the upstairs level of the house – in fact, it was quite an exception that we were shown any part of the interior of the house at all. Langdon family descendants spend their summers here, so the house is not open to the public. In the backyard, there is a barn full of materials belonging to the Mark Twain Studies Department of Elmira College – books, photographs, etc.

Next, Gretchen took us to see two graveyards. The first one was Woodlawn Cemetery, where the Langdon and Clemens families are buried. (Many of the Beecher family are buried here as well. Their graves are not individually marked – one large stone collectively identifies them.) We spent some time walking around the stones, reading whose was whose, and learning more about how they were all interred. Ossip Gabrilowitsch, Sam's son-in-law, had requested to be buried at Sam's feet, and he was. Clara, Ossip's wife, had a granite monument to the two men built in 1937, a year after she was widowed. It is twelve feet high – a twain high, with a fathom marker inside of the twain marker – and has bronze portraits of Sam and Ossip above it. Among the people buried here are Olivia, Sam, Susy, Clara, Jean, Ossip, Nina (Clara and Ossip's only daughter), Susan and Theodore Crane, Ida and Charles Langdon (Olivia's brother and his wife), their children, and the Langdon grandparents.

The second graveyard we saw was the town's

Catholic graveyard, in which Catherine Leary is buried. She went by the name Katy Leary, and she was the maid who worked for the Clemens family for thirty years – until just after Sam died, in 1910. She was originally from Elmira, and Olivia hired her in the drawing room of her parents' house in the summer of 1880.

Katy was just seventeen years old then, and this was to be her first job away from home. She was excited at the prospect of such independence, and impressed with how beautiful and quiet Olivia seemed. Olivia was called into the drawing room to meet Katy, and she came into the room dressed all in white. Katy liked her right away. Olivia liked her back; she wanted to know if there was anything in particular that Katy wanted in her new position, and was impressed with her requests. Katy wanted her own room, and permission to attend church every Sunday. Of course her requests were granted. Did Katy have any concerns about the location of her job in the winter? Yes – her mother was worried about her going so far away from home. No problem – Olivia's response to hearing this was to go and visit Katy's mother personally.

By the time Katy Leary retired, she had nursed one Clemens daughter on her deathbed, buried another to spare Sam having to do so, and enjoyed thirty years of meeting famous people, traveling to Europe, and going home to her family in the summertime. She then went home to Elmira permanently, and ran a boardinghouse for the rest of her life. Our next stop on the tour was therefore Katy Leary Park, near the former site of her boardinghouse. The park is a playground for children, with a swing set and a seesaw.

We then said thank you and good-bye to

Gretchen, and went out to dinner at the Pierce-Arrow Restaurant in Elmira. The food was excellent, inexpensive, and the price of the meal included an appetizer and a dessert. The surroundings were very elegant and quiet. The place is named for the automobile, one of which was on display in a separate outbuilding.

After dinner, we went on to meet Mark, the archivist of the Mark Twain Room in the Gannett-Tripp Learning Center at Elmira College. (This means that we went to a beautiful, wood-paneled room in the College's library where some original Twain materials are kept.) Mark showed us some books that the author owned and in which he had written when he gave them to a Quarry Farm employee by the name of John Lewis. Mr. Lewis, a former slave, had saved the lives of Ida Langdon and her baby when her horse started to run away, while pulling her buggy, at breakneck speed down Quarry Farm Road. Ida was going home after visiting her in-laws at the Farm. Sam and Theodore ran down the hill in horror – expecting to find Ida and her baby dead – but instead found John Lewis holding her horse still, with his wagon blocking its path. He had stopped it just in time.

The Langdons forgave all of his debts, gave him a party, and Sam presented him with some of his own copies of his novels – with money clipped to the inscribed pages. Those were just some of the wonderful things that Mark (the archivist) showed us. The visit went on and on while he showed us anything and everything that we wanted to see. Finally, we thanked him and went back to the Mark Twain Motor Inn for the night. I will spare the reader any description of that motel.

The next morning, Ernest drove us to see an old,

boarded up train station. This was the station at which the Clemens family got out every summer when they came to Elmira, and it was brand new when Sam first saw it in August of 1868. That was when he came for his first visit to meet all of the Langdons – and when he told his new friend Charles that he hoped to marry his sister, Olivia. Charles ordered him out of the house on the spot, but Sam managed (as expected) to stay for two weeks – by falling on the carpet and hitting his head on the way out the door. Olivia rushed him back inside, and the rest is history.

We proceeded on to the scene of the alleged fall: Park Street. There, we saw a pathetic site/sight. Where the old Langdon family mansion once stood, we beheld a hideous strip mall. It was small, diagonally situated, and just plain ugly. The mansion was torn down in 1939 to help pull Elmira out of the Great Depression – with a depressing replacement. There is a plaque on the corner of the lot, explaining all of this. Sam and Olivia were married here on February 2, 1870, and from here they went on to their new home in Buffalo, New York.

Across the street stands the Park Church, where we went to meet Eleanor. She showed us all around the place, inside and out. It was planned in 1871, and it replaced an earlier building of inadequate size. The church as an entity was first founded in 1846 by abolitionists, as the Independent Congregational Church. Thomas Kennicot Beecher ran the Park Church until his death in 1900. It is a huge building with no bell – a feature that made Mark Twain very happy – and a statue outside of its venerable first preacher. Inside we saw a beautiful wood-paneled meeting hall with balconies on both sides, a parlor, and a billiards room. Beecher would play in here and talk with members of his congregation. The parlor is especially nice – it is a carpeted room with Victorian furniture, all in pristine condition, with portraits of Olivia Lewis Langdon and Jervis Langdon (Mark Twain's in-laws), and a mandolin that Harriet Beecher Stowe had sent to her brother, the Reverend Thomas Beecher. The tour went on and on until we had seen every last room in the church, and then we thanked Eleanor and left.

This concluded our field trip, except for the long drive home. We had a great time, and wrote thank-you notes when we got back to Hartford. I have not given the full names of our hosts out of consideration for their privacy, should they value it. I will say, however, that they were all excellent – gracious and eminently knowledgeable.

Reading List

Historic interpreters not only attend lectures, guide-training classes, go on field trips and see movies, but we also read books both by and about Mark Twain. We never stop learning about him, even after training and becoming "seasoned" guides. Here is a list of some of my favorite reading material.

1. Mark Twain, *The Innocents Abroad*, 1870.
2. Charles Neider, Editor, *The Complete Short Stories of Mark Twain*, Doubleday Publishing, Inc., 1957.
3. *Mark Twain in Hartford*, copyright of the Mark Twain Memorial, Hartford, Connecticut, 1958.
4. Robert D. Jerome and Herbert A. Wisbey, Jr., *Mark Twain in Elmira*, Elmira Quality Printers, Inc., 1977.
5. J. Hurley Hagood and Roberta Roland Hagood, *Hannibal: Mark Twain's Town*, Jostens Publishing, 1988.
6. Doris Bernadette, Editor, Henry R. Martin, Illustrator, *Mark Twain: Wit and Wisecracks*, Peter Pauper Press, Inc., 1961.
7. Alex Ayres, Editor, *The Wit and Wisdom of Mark Twain*, Penguin Books U.S.A., Inc., 1987.
8. Bernard DeVoto, Editor, *Letters From the Earth: Uncensored Writings by Mark Twain*, Harper & Row, Publishers, 1991.
9. William Dean Howells, *My Mark Twain*, Harper and Brothers, Publishers, 1910.
10. Charles Neider, Editor, *Papa: An Intimate Biography of Mark Twain by His Thirteen-Year-Old Daughter Susy*, Doubleday and

Company, 1985.
11. Clara Langdon Clemens Gabrilowitsch, *My Father, Mark Twain*, 1931.
12. Mark Twain, *The Adventures of Tom Sawyer*, 1876.
13. Mark Twain, *The Adventures of Huckleberry Finn*, 1884.
14. Mark Twain, *Tom Sawyer Abroad*, 1894.
15. Mark Twain, *Tom Sawyer, Detective*, 1896.
16. Mark Twain, *The Prince and the Pauper*, 1882.
17. Mark Twain, *Pudd'nhead Wilson*, 1894.

Some of these books are out of print. Most can be found in bookstores. The Mark Twain House gift shop stocks all titles by and related to the author that are currently in print.

Part Three:
The Questions People Ask…

Questions…and Answers

The following is a list of questions which visitors have asked at the Mark Twain House. It is a collection that I have compiled from conversations with other guides as well as with members of my own tour groups. The identities of these questioners are either unknown or kept secret to protect the guilty. This is necessary and good – no one will be able to claim libel, insult, injury, or royalties. For many of these questions, comment is reserved. Sometimes, however, it is thrown in, just for fun. In other instances, it is provided as a serious answer to a thoughtful question. Topping the list is the guides' all-time favorite question.

Did Mark Twain work as a Mississippi River steamboat pilot while he lived here in Hartford, Connecticut?
No, the commute would have been too much for him.

Were Mark Twain and Harriet Beecher Stowe lovers?
She was 24 years older than he was.

So – where did Sam and Harriet keep their slaves?
They were abolitionists!!!! They were opposed to slavery.

Could you tell me…what is the difference between a servant and a slave?
Slaves can't quit. They also don't get paid.

What the question you get asked most here?
That's the one.

The Visitor Experience at the Mark Twain House

Is he writing there now?

Is the phone still connected?

How high are the ceilings?

Why can't we sit on the furniture?

Didn't one of the girls die?
They all died. I'll tell you when and in what order as the tour continues.

Does the speaking tube system still work?
It's disconnected.

What's behind that door?
This refers to the stenciled one in the front hall, under the staircase.
Answer: another staircase.

Is that the original wallpaper?
After you've just told your group that it's a reproduction.

What's the square footage of this house?
We would have to ask the curator to check the architectural plans of the house, drawn up in the summer of 1994 by several architectural students and their professor.

*You mean Sam and Olivia slept **together** – in the same bed – they did that in those days?*
Sure – how do you think couples had any children?!

In the library: *"Oh, I get it – <u>this</u> is Mark Twain's house!"* said a father.

The Visitor Experience at the Mark Twain House

"The weather is here – wish you were all beautiful."
– postcard from a guide touring some other Mark Twain related historic site.

Did he ever publish anything under the name Samuel L. Clemens?
No…that was what he had a penname for.

"Mm, Hm – Mama said so." These words followed every sentence spoken by the guide. She never found out what prompted that.

A museum room exhibit in the basement once featured Tiffany lamps and, as the tour mentions, Louis Comfort Tiffany led the decoration project of Olivia's house. Yet a visitor once asked, angrily, *"What are all these lamps doing here?"*

"Are you Mark Twain's daughter?" asked a 5th grader.

What happened to Mark Twain's wife after he died?
She predeceased him.
Yes, but what happened to her after he died?!
They were excommunicated from heaven to purgatory, where they existed happily ever. This was like Eden to Sam, because Olivia was there with him. Sometimes the best answer to an illogical question is a logical one.

Was Harriet [Beecher Stowe] Clara's sister?

Was there an underground tunnel between the houses?
No. The Civil War, slavery, and the Underground

Railroad system were no longer in progress by the time that these houses were built. No tunnel was needed.

Was Mark Twain a juggler?

Who is this Sam you keep referring to?
Some people just won't listen to the guide, no matter what.

Often, the moment you pause to breathe between recitations of facts, a visitor will ask a question about the exact thing you have just finished discussing.

Is it true that all of his hair turned white at once when he learned of the death of one of his daughters?

How did the typesetter work?
It didn't. Not for more than three minutes at a time. No one, not even present-day engineers, can answer this question with any more detail.

Evening walk-through: middle-aged, slightly drunken male visitors have been heard to say that they know Mark Twain. And I know Susan B. Anthony.

A visitor who once spent an entire day in the Billiards Room assembling the original table knew what I would talk about in that room, but thoughtfully let me say it.

What happened to the house after the Clemens family sold it?

The Bissel family – the owners of the Hartford Fire

Insurance Company, now ITT Hartford – bought the house in 1903. It would have been a short ride to work for the father, just down Farmington Avenue to the fork with Asylum Street. They redecorated the house, putting a large fountain in the conservatory, and parquet floors in the drawing and dining rooms. Olivia had had wall-to-wall carpeting in those rooms. The Bissel family lived here for fourteen years.

After that, they rented it out for five years to the Kingswood School for boys, which used the library room as a study hall. They didn't change anything inside – they just occupied the place. They did, however, level off the wooded area at the lower end of the ravine for a playing field. Today, it is a grassy, open area. In 1922, they left, moved to their present location in West Hartford, and merged with the Oxford School for girls.

At that point, the Bissel family sold the house to a coal company. It used the servants' wing as office space and stored its things in crates and boxes throughout the rest of the house. They didn't cause any damage or redecorate.

Then, in 1927, Katherine Seymour Day returned to Nook Farm after 30 years of travel, and moved into the Harriet Beecher Stowe house. She saw that this house, which she remembered so well from the 1890s, when she lived in it with her family, was for sale. (Her mother and Olivia had attended college together, and become friends.) This house was then threatened with demolition. She made up her mind to save it. It took two years, but she managed to summon a group of wealthy West Hartford families to finance her purchase. The deal was closed in 1929, with a huge mortgage. She was then named the chairperson in charge of the committee to pay off the debt.

She decided to rent the upper two floors out as apartments. That meant that twentieth-century bathroom fixtures would have to replace nineteenth-century ones, and that the walls would have to be painted white. This would lead to further complications at restoration time, but was unavoidable.

The first floor – with the exception of the guest suite – was rented out to the Hartford Public Library. This is how the Mark Twain Branch of the Hartford Public Library came to be established. The library did a lot of damage. It painted the upper areas of the front hall white, covering the red and blue stencilings, and knocked out the walnut carvings in the bookcases of the library room.

After twenty-six years – 1929 to 1955 – the mortgage was paid off. The restoration project could begin. It took twenty years, until 1975. Paint was scraped off of the walls all over the house to find out how they were first decorated. Once the stencilings were revealed, smithcrafters trained in museum restoration were hired to affix new reproductions onto the appropriate walls. Some examples of the original work have been left under plexiglass for visitors to see. In the nursery, the mantelpiece had to be ripped away from the wall in order to reveal the only surviving scrap of the original wallpaper. Once the frog nursery rhyme had been found, a sample was taken to an archive with old, Victorian wallpaper catalogues. When a match was found, a sufficient quantity of wallpaper was order and later installed.

With the exception of Susy's room, the restoration was almost complete in 1974, when tours began to be offered. Meanwhile, the process is a never-ending one. Whenever it becomes possible to restore another section of the house, it is done. This will continue until the entire museum recreates the condition of the house when the Clemens family lived here.

People often remember visiting friends when there were apartments on the second and third floors of the house. One man remembered delivering groceries to the tenants.

Is this real?
No – it's an illusion, a hologram, a figment of your imagination. The term used in a historic house museum is "original".

"This is Mark Twain's bed, and guess who slept in it?" A little kid looked at the four angels on the bedposts and said "The Pope?"

Do you change the light bulbs in here?
Yes. We just don't use bright ones. It is supposed to be dim inside.

"I could keep you here in hysterics for hours, but we must go on with the tour.
"This is a favorite line of our favorite, most veteran guide. He uses it with people who don't show any signs of moving on to the next room.

At the front doorstep: *Is this stone from a riverbed?*
It's actually brownstone, cut like a split log – jaggedly and incorrectly – long before people knew how to cut it.

Someone saw a curator's catalogue tag hanging from a quilt and said, *"Oh, it's still got its price tag on it."* Its true purpose was promptly explained.

High school sophomores – one asked, *"Where did Mark go?"* I caught myself in time and refrained from saying, "He's dead!"

The ornament of a house is the freaks who friendly it. This is a Ralph Waldo Emerson quote that was garbled by a guide who had reeled it off too many times.

A woman appeared out of nowhere while the boss and two guides were closing the house and asked, *"Was this house built on a boat?"* Afterward, a guide said, "Yeah, the USS *Lexington*."

Are the rugs we're standing on original?

Oh, it must play the tune from The Godfather*!* a visitor said, on hearing that the original music box had played arias from German and Italian operas. Hmmm, hm, hm, hmmm, hm, hm, hmmm.

The museum room had been closed for a leak or, rather, severe flood in the Mark Twain House basement. A guide who didn't know this reached the end of the tour and said, *"And now we will be going down into the museum room..."*
Out popped another guide from the second floor to say, *"You won't be going down to the museum room."* The guide calmly resumed, *"We won't be going down to the museum room."*

A man wanted to know if the nursery dollhouse was a model of Sam's boyhood home in Hannibal, Missouri.

The Visitor Experience at the Mark Twain House

Did Mark Twain have anything to do with the OK Corral?

When did you move these houses here?
We didn't – they were built right here.

Did they dig this cellar especially for the museum room?
It is part of the foundation that supports this house.

Why are there three doorbells here?

So is this room exactly the way it was when the Clemens family lived here?
We were in the basement of the house, which was then set up as a museum room.

During the Christmas walk-through, a guide who was standing in the Mahogany Guest Suite overhead one visitor asking another: *"So is this the room where Elvis died?"*

A visitor and a guide, both of whom were from Utah but discovered that fact later…
Visitor: *Did Mark Twain have more than one wife?*
Guide: *No, he wasn't a Mormon.*

Did Mark Twain have Tourette Syndrome?
No, he swore on purpose.

Is this the original house?
Of course it is!

Is there a book I can buy with a written tour of the Mark Twain House?
Yes. This one.

Part Four:
Visitor Services of All Kinds

Visitor Services and Other Facts

The fact that consumers like to know what is being offered for their consumption in universally understood. Therefore, this section is devoted to explaining just that on behalf of the Mark Twain House.

The Mark Twain House was the home of the author Samuel Langhorne Clemens and his family for seventeen years. Sam – Mark Twain – was the most famous American writer of the nineteenth century. He and his wife, Olivia Louise Langdon Clemens, raised their three daughters here. This was a very happy place, and visitors are given a sense of that in our tours.

Guided tours, evening walk-throughs, carriage house rentals, Christmas walk-throughs, story-tellings, Mark Twain Days activities, symposia and a gift shop are offered at the Mark Twain House.

Mark Twain once said that if someone asked him what his exact address was, he couldn't give an answer, as he did not know his street number. As tour guides, however, we are required to remember it:

The Mark Twain House
351 Farmington Avenue
Hartford, Connecticut 06105
U.S.A.

There are several telephone numbers/extensions – Sam would have been outraged by this! They can be accessed by a recorded voice mail system, which includes the Visitor Center Administrator, the Gift Shop, directions, and opening hours. The main number is:

(860) 247-0998

In addition to all of this, the Mark Twain House is online. Its website address is https://www.marktwainhouse.org – complete with an educational kit for teachers, and a description of its other services.

Tourist guidebooks refer to the buildings surrounding and including the Mark Twain House as Nook Farm. This was the name of Mark Twain's neighborhood in the late nineteenth century. There are now only five remaining of the original eighteen buildings. Facing them from Farmington Avenue, one can see, from left to right, the Stowe-Day Library, the Harriet Beecher Stowe House, the carriage house for the Stowe-Day Library, the carriage house for the Mark Twain House, and the Mark Twain House. They continue to stand on the exact sites on which they were built.

The Visitor Experience at the Mark Twain House

Harriet Beecher Stowe – author of *Uncle Tom's Cabin* – and Mark Twain – author of *The Adventures of Huckleberry Finn* – lived across the yard from one another for seventeen years during the late nineteenth century. Mrs. Stowe lived in her retirement home with her husband and adult twin daughters; Twain and his wife raised their three daughters in their family home. Both authors wrote in these houses and were world-famous while they lived in them.

The Visitor Center and Gift Shop

For a long time, the carriage house to the Stowe-Day Library, owned by the Stowe-Day Foundation, served as the joint Visitor Center for both the Harriet Beecher Stowe House and the Mark Twain House.

Then, in August of 1993, a meeting was held. During the course of this meeting, it was announced to the guides that the two museums were, essentially, getting a divorce. They would no longer operate a joint visitor center. Six weeks later, everything was in place at the Mark Twain House.

Plans existed for an elaborate new building that would house the entire staff of the museum, thus freeing every room in the Mark Twain House for restoration and education, and it was finally completed in 2003.

The visitor center can be found behind the carriage house of the Mark Twain House. Visitors can park down below both buildings and either walk up a staircase to its entrance, or wheel up a ramp to the right of the stairs. Parking is free.

To access it by car, enter the driveway to its

parking lot from Farmington Avenue, then turn left (the parking lot on the right is for an apartment complex). You will know that you are in the right place when you see the athletic field for Hartford Public High School. Also, signs are posted to indicate precisely where to find it.

As you go inside, you will find artwork about the author's life and times, and the gift shop on the right. Continue past it, and there are rest rooms and a coat area to the right, followed by the ticket desk.

The Visitor Experience at the Mark Twain House

Around the corner from the ticket desk is a museum room with many artifacts from Mark Twain's printing and writing careers, including the Paige Typesetting Machine. Across from this room are 2 rooms. One is a small theater for movies about Mark Twain and his family. The other is a large auditorium, which holds lectures from visiting scholars. A large open space between these rooms contains a piano and some tables, where catered events are held, some of which precede lectures.

The gift shop is a large, modern room that offers every sort of book by and about Mark Twain, plus snacks, coffee, t-shirts, scarves, ties, socks, jewelry, hatpins, bookmarks, magnets, toys, and all kinds of knick-knacks.

The artwork out in the hallway is a lot of fun. It includes a large, colorful statue of a frog, which commemorates the story of *The Jumping Frog of Calaveras County*, and a sculpture that depicts Mark Twain with many of the characters from his novels and other books, including Joan of Ark (a biography that he was most proud of).

There are also benches to sit on, and many other pieces of artwork to look at, plus a plaque detailing who the donors are that provided funds for this building and for further restorations of the house.

Upstairs, there is much more. There is a wide staircase and an elevator that will take the visitor to the upper level of the visitor center. The staircase is straight ahead of the ticket desk, to the left of the auditorium. The elevator is at the back of the large room where catered food is served.

The upper level includes a large museum room of artifacts that relate to Mark Twain's family life. This includes clothing, toys, housewares, and artifacts owned by Olivia, Suzy, Clara, and Jean, plus a slide show of photographs of Ossip and Nina.

Continue on down the hall, over a balcony that overlooks the catering hall, and enjoy framed artwork along the way.

At the end of this hallway is a café with another small gift shop. The Nook Farm Café offers sandwiches, salads, sushi, fruit, desserts, chocolates, and drinks…and free wi-fi.

Glass doors lead out of it to the Carriage House, which serves as another venue for events, such as famous authors who have come to showcase their new books.

Tours are led by historic interpreters through the family part of the house, which makes up the bulk of it, plus the fully restored servants' wing.

Tours are conducted by Historic Interpreters, who have studied Mark Twain, his life, his writings, and the house. These individuals are paid, so they are not docents, who provide tours for free, as volunteers. A historic interpreter differs from a tour guide in that guides merely show visitors around a place, while interpreters draw connections between people and events, and between objects and people.

Tickets for either or both sections are offered. The admission rates vary, with prices for adults, seniors, and children (free to children under 6).

The hours at the Mark Twain House are:

Sundays:	Noon – 5 p.m.
Mondays:	9:30 a.m. – 5 p.m.
Tuesdays:	9:30 a.m. – 5 p.m.[†]
Wednesdays:	9:30 a.m. – 5 p.m.
Thursdays:	9:30 a.m. – 5 p.m.
Fridays:	9:30 a.m. – 5 p.m.
Saturdays:	9:30 a.m. – 5 p.m.

The museum is open on July 4th and on all Monday holidays, and is closed on New Year's Day, Easter Sunday, Thanksgiving Day, Christmas Eve, and Christmas Day.

From late November through the beginning of January, the Mark Twain House is decorated as if for Christmas. Sam and Olivia traveled in Heidelberg, Germany, in the 1870s, and adopted various holiday traditions there, including having a Christmas tree.

Special group rates are available for student tours and other group tours (minimum – 10 visitors), provided that such tours are pre-arranged.

Although the house is open until 5 p.m., it is not possible to sign up for a tour after 4 p.m., because the tours take a full hour apiece, and the museum closes

---

[†] Open on Tuesdays only in May, June, July, August, September, October, and December.

The Visitor Experience at the Mark Twain House

at 5 p.m. The only way to see the house is through a guided tour. No one may walk through unattended.

As for the admission rate for persons aged five years or younger, it depends on an individual's point of view. Each adult must consider whether or not she or he ought to bring a young person on a tour, and how that young person is likely to behave. If a child becomes a distraction* to the guide and to other members of a tour, the adult who brought that child will be asked to take the child out…unless that adult volunteers to do so. No refund shall be provided to this adult.

Anyone who wishes to place a bet consisting of the price of their own admission to the museum on a child at the Mark Twain Casino is welcome to do so.

---

* Distractions range from crying constantly at all decibels, to eating food or drinking anything, to playing with toys, to disappearing into the hallway or into another room during the tour.

Additional Services

Other services include carriage house rentals, symposia, ghost tours, mystery nights, writing sessions in the library room of the Mark Twain House, and holiday tours.

For more detail, visit the Mark Twain House website: https://marktwainhouse.org/events/

Events are held year-round. These include a series called **Mark My Words**, for authors, and **The Trouble Begins at 5:30**, named for Mark Twain's lectures given in San Francisco, when he had no idea what he would talk about. His plan was to pack the seats and wing it. The people who speak at today's events have put more planning into their presentations, however! They talk about Mark Twain, providing scholarly insight into his work style, habits, and other efforts. For more information on this, visit the website at: https://marktwainhouse.org/events/category/the-trouble-begins-at-530/

Memberships can be purchased, which entitle visitors to discounts on ticket fees to the house and to events, plus sales in the gift shop.

About the Author

Stephanie C. Fox, J.D. is a historian, author, and editor. She is a graduate of William Smith College and the University of Connecticut School of Law.

She runs an editing and publishing service called *QueenBeeEdit*, found at www.queenbeeedit.com, which caters to politicians, scientists, and others.

Her imprint is *QueenBeeBooks*.

Ms. Fox has written several books on a variety of topics, including the effects of human overpopulation on the environment, Asperger's, cats, and travel to Kuwait and Hawai'i.

www.ingramcontent.com/pod-product-compliance
Lightning Source LLC
Chambersburg PA
CBHW070118110526
44587CB00015BA/2356